I0014296

Future of Digital Marketing: Harnessing AI, Social Media and Data Driven Strategies for Personal & Professional Growth

Jayant Deshmukh

Published by Jayant Deshmukh, 2025.

Table of Contents

Disclaimer

The information provided in this book is for general informational and educational purposes only. Every effort has been made to ensure the accuracy and reliability of the content at the time of publication. However, the author and publisher make no representations or warranties regarding the completeness, accuracy, or suitability of the information contained in this book.

The tools, applications, and techniques mentioned are subject to changes in availability, pricing, and functionality by their respective developers or organizations. Readers are advised to conduct their own research and exercise discretion before using any tool or implementing any recommendations.

The author and publisher shall not be held liable for any damages, losses, or adverse consequences arising from the use or misuse of the information provided herein. Any reliance you place on the information in this book is strictly at your own risk.

This book includes references to third-party tools, websites, and applications, which are used solely for informational purposes. The inclusion of such references does not imply endorsement or affiliation with the respective developers or organizations.

This book does not serve as financial, legal, or technical advice. For specific concerns or personalized recommendations, readers are encouraged to consult professionals in the relevant fields.

By reading this book, you acknowledge that you have read, understood, and agree to the terms of this disclaimer.

FUTURE OF DIGITAL MARKETING: HARNESSING AI, SOCIAL MEDIA AND DATA DRIVEN STRATEGIES FOR PERSONAL & PROFESSIONAL GROWTH

First edition. FEBRUARY 16, 2025.

Written by Jayant Deshmukh.

About the Author

Jayant Deshmukh is a visionary leader at the intersection of technology and human potential. Certified Project Management Professional (PMP) and an AI expert with a wealth of experience in driving digital transformation initiatives across the globe. With over 16 years in the IT industry, Jayant has had the privilege of working with numerous banks and financial institutions worldwide, helping them navigate the complexities of technological evolution and embrace the future of AI and digitalization. His expertise lies in understanding how emerging technologies, like AI, can revolutionize business models, streamline operations, and create sustainable wealth.

Jayant's professional journey has taken him to multiple countries, where he collaborated with multinational corporations (MNCs) in various sectors. This international exposure has equipped him with a deep understanding of diverse geographies, cultures, and the unique challenges faced by individuals, businesses, and societies around the world. Through his work with these corporations, he has gained valuable insights into how people, regardless of their location, share common aspirations and desires for growth, success, and financial independence. His experience allows him to design AI-driven strategies that cater to the specific needs of individuals and businesses across the globe, helping them build better lives and brighter futures.

Beyond the corporate world, Jayant has been **deeply involved in digital marketing and social media campaigns for Entrepreneurs, Social and Political organizations**, utilizing AI-powered strategies to understand public sentiment and drive impactful social campaigns. His experience in working closely with **political parties, grassroots organizations, and digital advocacy groups** has given him an unparalleled understanding of the **common man's challenges** and how **technology can be harnessed for societal progress**.

Books Authored by Jayant Deshmukh

Jayant has penned several impactful books that reflect his expertise, passion, and vision for empowering individuals and professionals. Each book is crafted with a human touch, engaging storytelling, and actionable insights.

1. **Prompt Engineering - The Ultimate Guide for Success in Artificial Intelligence**

This definitive guide to AI prompt engineering offers a comprehensive introduction to AI interaction, helping both beginners and professionals harness AI's power. Packed with practical tools, insights, and examples, it empowers readers to leverage AI effectively in their daily and professional lives.

2. **Mastering the Art of Corporate Communication** Aimed at enhancing influence, collaboration, and leadership, this book explores 149 effective communication strategies essential for success in the corporate world. It provides actionable advice and real-life examples,

equipping readers to strengthen their communication skills and make an impact in any professional setting.

3. **Step by Step Guide to Overcome Corporate Politics** Through a practical and storytelling-driven approach, this book presents 105 proven techniques to navigate and resolve corporate politics. It helps readers manage office dynamics, avoid conflicts, and thrive in their professional journeys, all while maintaining authenticity and integrity.

4. **Digital Transformation in Banking & Finance: Unlocking the Power of 110 AI Tools to Revolutionize the Banking and Finance Industry** An in-depth exploration of how AI tools are transforming the banking and finance sectors, this book provides insights into 110 AI-powered tools that enhance productivity, improve customer experiences, and drive innovation. It's a must-read for financial professionals looking to embrace AI.

5. **Building a Career in AI: A Practical Guide for Aspiring Professionals** A motivational and inspiring guide for individuals starting or transitioning into AI careers. This book offers real-life examples, practical advice, and actionable steps, serving as a roadmap for aspiring AI professionals to succeed in this dynamic field.

6. **AI Tools for Everyone: 119 Best AI Tools to Master Everyday Tasks** This book introduces readers to 119 AI tools designed to improve efficiency and productivity in everyday tasks. From personal use to business applications, Jayant demonstrates how these tools simplify processes and help users accomplish more in less time, making AI accessible to all.

7. **10x Productivity Hacks: Unlocking the Secrets of AI to Boost Productivity, Efficiency and Transform Your Life** A practical guide that shares powerful strategies and tools to dramatically enhance

productivity. It offers actionable insights for individuals looking to maximize their output while maintaining a healthy work-life balance.

8. Nurturing Growth Mindset: A Parent's Guide for Raising Innovative, Adaptive and Empowered Children This book is a heartfelt guide for parents, blending Jayant's professional acumen with his personal experiences as a parent. It offers insights into equipping children with the skills, resilience, and mindset needed to thrive in the AI-driven world.

9. AI Revolution in Medicine & HealthCare: Digital Transformation through Artificial Intelligence

An in-depth exploration of how AI is revolutionizing the Medicine and HealthCare sector, this book is must-read for healthcare professionals looking to embrace AI.

10. Artificial Intelligence for Financial Freedom: 100 Passive Income Strategies to Build Wealth in the Digital Era

To harness the power of AI to create sustainable passive income streams and achieve financial independence in today's digital-first world.

An **author, speaker, and thought leader**, Jayant is passionate about **helping businesses, professionals, and aspiring marketers** navigate the rapidly evolving **landscape of AI and digital marketing**. Through his books, lectures, and consulting work, he aims to empower individuals with **the knowledge and tools** they need to thrive in the **AI-driven digital era.**

In *Future of Digital Marketing: Harnessing AI, Social Media, and Data-Driven Strategies for Personal & Professional Growth*, Jayant distills years of experience, research, and real-world insights to help **businesses, entrepreneurs, and marketing professionals** unlock the **true potential of AI, automation, and data analytics.**

Jayant enjoys exploring new cultures, engaging in social initiatives, and contributing to the digital revolution.

Connect with Jayant Deshmukh on social media at :

https://www.instagram.com/jayantdeshmukhofficial/

https://www.linkedin.com/in/jayant-deshmukh-pmp/

https://www.facebook.com/jayantdeshmukh01

https://www.youtube.com/@jayantdeshm

https://www.threads.net/@jayantdeshmukhofficial

https://x.com/jayantdeshm

Prologue

In the last two decades, the world has transformed in ways we could have never imagined. I still remember the early days of digital marketing—when having a website was considered revolutionary, email marketing felt like magic, and social media was just an emerging trend. Fast forward to today, and we are witnessing an era where artificial intelligence, hyper-personalization, and automation are reshaping how businesses connect with consumers. Digital marketing has evolved from an experimental tactic to an indispensable strategy, and those who fail to adapt will be left behind.

The idea for this book was born out of my personal journey—having worked with multinational corporations, startups, entrepreneurs, and political organizations, I have seen firsthand how AI-driven digital marketing has become a game-changer. From banking to e-commerce, healthcare to entertainment, no industry has remained untouched by the digital revolution. Yet, amidst all the technological advancements, one thing remains constant: the need for businesses to engage, inspire, and connect with their customers on a human level.

The Evolution of Digital Marketing: A Brief Journey

To understand where we are heading, we must first look back at how far we have come. The early 2000s marked the birth of digital marketing as we know it today. Search engines like Google changed the way businesses attracted customers, and SEO became the foundation of online visibility. Soon after, social media giants like Facebook, Twitter, and LinkedIn emerged, redefining engagement and community building.

Then came the era of smartphones. With mobile devices dominating internet usage, brands were compelled to optimize their content for a new wave of users who demanded real-time information, personalized experiences, and seamless interactions. Digital ads became smarter, algorithms became more powerful, and consumer expectations skyrocketed.

Fast forward to the present, and artificial intelligence has taken center stage. AI-powered chatbots, predictive analytics, voice search, and machine learning-driven content creation are shaping a future where marketing is no longer just about selling products—it's about delivering experiences that are tailor-made for every individual.

Why This Book Matters Now More Than Ever

We are at a critical juncture. The rapid integration of AI in digital marketing has left businesses and professionals with two choices—adapt and thrive or resist and fade into obscurity. This book is not just about theories and trends; it's about actionable insights that will help you future-proof your business and career in the ever-changing digital landscape.

If you are a business owner, this book will guide you on leveraging AI-driven strategies to scale and remain competitive. If you are a marketer, you will learn how to use AI to make data-driven decisions, optimize campaigns, and engage your audience like never before. If you are an aspiring entrepreneur or a student stepping into this dynamic field, this book will serve as your roadmap to mastering digital marketing in the AI era.

How Businesses and Individuals Can Adapt

The fundamental question is—how do we navigate this transformation without losing the essence of marketing? Here's the key: embrace change, stay agile, and leverage AI as an enabler, not a replacement.

1. **Adopt AI-Driven Strategies** – AI is no longer a futuristic concept; it is here and now. Businesses must integrate AI-driven tools for audience segmentation, predictive analytics, and automation to stay relevant.
2. **Focus on Hyper-Personalization** – Gone are the days of generic marketing. Consumers expect brands to understand their needs, preferences, and behaviors. AI makes it possible to deliver personalized content, recommendations, and ads that resonate with individuals.
3. **Enhance Customer Experiences** – The brands that will win in the future are the ones that create seamless, engaging, and memorable customer experiences. AI-powered chatbots, virtual assistants, and voice search optimization will play a crucial role in delivering superior service.
4. **Invest in Continuous Learning** – The digital marketing landscape is evolving at an unprecedented pace. Professionals and business leaders must prioritize upskilling, staying updated on the latest AI trends, and adapting their strategies accordingly.
5. **Embrace Ethical Marketing and Data Privacy** – With AI-driven marketing comes the responsibility of ethical advertising and data protection. Businesses must ensure transparency, comply with regulations, and build trust with their audience.

Looking Ahead: The Future of Digital Marketing

Imagine a world where AI anticipates customer needs before they even express them, where voice assistants become the primary mode of search, and where virtual reality shopping experiences become the norm. The future of digital marketing is not about replacing humans with AI—it's about enhancing human creativity with AI's analytical power.

As we move toward 2030 and beyond, the way we approach marketing will continue to evolve. The brands that succeed will be the ones that strike a balance between technological advancements and authentic human connections.

Final Thoughts

This book is my attempt to bridge the gap between AI-driven digital marketing strategies and real-world implementation. It is a guide for businesses, marketers, and individuals who want to thrive in an AI-powered world without losing sight of what truly matters—understanding and connecting with people.

So, as you turn the pages of this book, remember that digital marketing is not just about technology; it's about transformation. It's about how we, as businesses and individuals, adapt, innovate, and lead in an era where AI is no longer an option—it's the future.

Welcome to the journey of mastering digital marketing in the age of AI. Let's dive in.

Introduction

I still remember the time when businesses—big and small—relied on newspapers, television ads, and billboards to spread their message. Marketing was straightforward but extremely limited. If you wanted to reach a large audience, you needed deep pockets to afford prime-time TV spots or full-page ads in national dailies. There was no way to track if people actually saw your ad, let alone whether they engaged with it.

Fast forward to today, and the marketing landscape has undergone a complete transformation. With the advent of social media, artificial intelligence, and data-driven insights, marketing is no longer about pushing products—it's about creating experiences, building relationships, and engaging with audiences on a personal level.

My journey into digital marketing was not just about keeping up with trends; it was about **leveraging technology to create real impact**—whether it was for businesses, individuals, or even political movements.

And trust me, I have seen firsthand how digital marketing can **shape businesses, define personal brands, and even win elections!**

The Power of Digital in Politics: My Experience with AAP & BRS

One of the most intriguing aspects of my career has been working with **political parties to establish and strengthen their digital presence**. Traditional political campaigns relied heavily on rallies, newspaper advertisements, and word-of-mouth. But in the digital age, **social media became the new battleground**—a place where perceptions were formed, narratives were controlled, and voter sentiments were influenced.

Building AAP's Digital Presence

When I was involved with the **Aam Aadmi Party (AAP)** during their early days, they were an emerging force, challenging the traditional political setup in India. Their success was deeply rooted in **grassroots mobilization**, but they lacked the digital presence required to engage with a tech-savvy, younger electorate.

Our goal was simple:

1. **Amplify AAP's Message** – We needed to reach millions of people without relying on mainstream media.
2. **Create Viral, Engaging Content** – Politics was no longer about speeches and manifestos; it was about storytelling.
3. **Engage Directly with the Public** – Traditional parties relied on spokespersons, but we wanted a direct conversation with voters.

We started by creating **highly targeted content**—short videos, social media posts, and infographics—explaining AAP's policies and vision in simple, relatable terms. **Facebook, Twitter, and YouTube became our battlegrounds**.

One of our most successful campaigns was when we leveraged **real-time engagement** on Twitter. Every time a political opponent attacked AAP, we countered with facts, short videos, and interactive Q&A sessions. This level of responsiveness made the party **look transparent, accountable, and in touch with the people**.

Within months, we saw exponential growth in AAP's digital reach. Their Twitter handle, which had a few thousand followers, soon crossed a million. **Videos explaining policies in 60 seconds** started getting shared widely, reaching even those who were not politically inclined.

This was **not just about visibility—it was about trust-building.** And trust, in politics, is everything.

Strengthening BRS's Digital Strategy

My experience with **Bharat Rashtra Samithi (BRS)** was equally exciting but vastly different. Unlike AAP, which was a new party needing recognition, BRS (formerly TRS) had **an established base but lacked digital sophistication.**

Here, the challenge was:

1. **Reaching out to a younger demographic** – The party needed to connect with first-time voters.
2. **Shifting from traditional to modern campaign strategies** – Digital had to complement their on-ground presence.
3. **Managing crisis communication** – In politics, narratives change every day, and social media is a double-edged sword.

We introduced **AI-powered sentiment analysis tools** to track public perception in real time. This allowed the party to understand what issues people cared about and respond accordingly.

A key breakthrough was the **WhatsApp voter outreach campaign.** Unlike social media, where algorithms limit organic reach, WhatsApp allowed **direct, unfiltered communication with voters.** Through localized video messages, voice notes, and interactive polls, we engaged people in a way that traditional rallies never could.

The results?

- A **30% increase in youth engagement on Instagram and Twitter.**
- Over **5 million views on campaign videos in a matter of**

weeks.

- Real-time damage control whenever misinformation was spread online.

Digital marketing had turned into **a powerful weapon in political strategy**, and I was fortunate to be part of this transformation.

Personal Branding in the Digital Era: Helping Businesses & Individuals Shine

Beyond politics, I have worked closely with **entrepreneurs, executives, and businesses** to **build their personal brands online.**

Today, **your digital footprint is your resume.** Whether you are an entrepreneur, an artist, or a business leader, people will Google you before they meet you. If your digital presence is weak, you are missing out on opportunities.

Let me share an interesting case study.

Helping a Young Entrepreneur Build Authority Online

A few years ago, I was approached by a **young startup founder** who had a fantastic product but no credibility in the industry. He was struggling to raise funding because **investors didn't trust him as a thought leader.**

We devised a **three-step strategy** to establish his authority online:

1. **Content-Driven Branding** – He started publishing well-researched LinkedIn articles about industry trends.
2. **Podcast & Video Presence** – Instead of relying on written content alone, we created a **YouTube channel and a podcast** where he interviewed industry leaders.
3. **Social Media Engagement** – Rather than just posting, we

engaged with influencers, joined Twitter conversations, and hosted LinkedIn live sessions.

Within a year, his LinkedIn followers grew from **1,200 to over 50,000**, and his articles started getting featured in industry publications. **Investors took notice, and he secured funding for his startup.**

This is the power of **personal branding** in the digital age. It's not about self-promotion; it's about **creating value, building trust, and positioning yourself as an authority in your field.**

The Digital Marketing Shift: From Traditional to AI-Driven Strategies

The **real game-changer** in digital marketing today is **Artificial Intelligence (AI).**

Gone are the days when digital marketing was just about running Facebook ads and SEO. Today, AI enables:

- **Hyper-personalized marketing** – AI predicts what a consumer wants before they even know it.
- **Automated content creation** – AI tools can write blogs, generate ads, and even create videos.
- **Predictive analytics** – AI can forecast which customers are most likely to convert.

Take Netflix as an example. The reason you keep binge-watching is because **AI recommends content tailored to your viewing habits.** Imagine applying that same principle to marketing—offering the right product, at the right time, to the right audience.

This is where the future is headed, and those who **adapt to AI-driven marketing strategies will dominate.**

Why This Book?

I wrote this book because **digital marketing is no longer an option—it's a necessity.**

Whether you are an entrepreneur, a marketer, a political strategist, or someone trying to build a personal brand, **you cannot ignore the digital landscape.**

This book will:

1. **Demystify AI-driven digital marketing** – Making it easy for anyone to understand and implement.
2. **Provide actionable strategies** – So you can apply them to your own business or brand.
3. **Prepare you for the future** – Because the way we market today will look very different in five years.

I have seen firsthand how **digital marketing has transformed industries, influenced elections, and built billion-dollar brands.** If you're ready to harness its power, let's dive in together.

" *The future of marketing belongs to those who embrace change, harness the power of AI, and create meaningful connections in a digital world. Adapt, innovate, and lead—because the only constant in this journey is evolution.*"

– Jayant Deshmukh

Chapter 1: The Evolution of Digital Marketing

From Traditional to Digital: A Quick Recap

Let's take a moment to step back in time. Picture yourself in the early 1990s. Marketing was a vastly different world—one dominated by television commercials, radio jingles, newspaper ads, and billboards towering over busy city streets. Businesses relied heavily on these methods, hoping their messages would reach the right audience. There was no way to track how many people actually saw an ad, engaged with it, or made a purchase because of it. Marketing decisions were often based on intuition, past experiences, and broad consumer trends rather than hard data.

Then, the internet arrived.

The mid-1990s marked the beginning of a digital revolution that changed everything. Businesses started experimenting with simple websites, emails replaced direct mail, and search engines like Yahoo! and AltaVista made it easier for consumers to find information online. Marketers quickly realized that **digital platforms allowed them to reach a global audience at a fraction of the cost of traditional advertising.**

The Turning Point: The Birth of Google and Digital Ads

When Google launched in 1998, it completely changed how people accessed information. Suddenly, businesses could be discovered not just through word-of-mouth or expensive TV spots but by simply appearing in search results. Soon after, **Google AdWords (now Google Ads) was introduced, allowing brands to bid for placement on search result pages.** This was a game-changer because, for the first time, advertisers could target specific keywords and track how many people clicked on their ads.

E-commerce also started to gain traction. **Amazon and eBay began reshaping consumer behavior**, showing that shopping didn't need to be limited to physical stores. With this shift, businesses realized they needed an online presence—not just as an option but as a necessity.

Key Milestones in Digital Marketing

Over the years, digital marketing has evolved in leaps and bounds. Let's explore some of the major milestones that have shaped today's digital landscape.

1. The Rise of SEO (Search Engine Optimization) – Early 2000s

As more businesses went online, competition for visibility skyrocketed. This led to the birth of **Search Engine Optimization (SEO), a technique aimed at improving website rankings on search engines like Google.** Marketers began understanding how Google's algorithms worked—favoring content-rich, keyword-optimized websites with relevant backlinks.

Real-Life Example: In the early 2000s, businesses like Moz and HubSpot emerged as leaders in the SEO space, offering tools and strategies to help brands improve their rankings. **Companies that adopted SEO early saw massive organic traffic growth, reducing their dependency on paid advertising.**

2. The Social Media Revolution – Mid-2000s

In the mid-2000s, social media transformed how businesses connected with consumers. Platforms like Facebook (2004), YouTube (2005), Twitter (2006), and later Instagram (2010) allowed brands to engage directly with audiences in real time.

Companies quickly realized the power of social media marketing. **Instead of relying solely on traditional ads, businesses could now create engaging content, interact with customers, and even handle customer service via social platforms.**

Real-Life Example: Coca-Cola's "Share a Coke" campaign in 2011 took social media by storm. By personalizing bottles with names and encouraging customers to share their experiences online, the brand saw a **7% increase in sales in the U.S. alone.**

3. The PPC (Pay-Per-Click) Advertising Boom – Late 2000s

With Google Ads gaining traction, paid digital advertising became mainstream. Businesses could now run targeted ads and **only pay when someone clicked on them.** This made marketing far more cost-effective than traditional ads, where businesses paid a fixed amount regardless of engagement.

Facebook Ads followed suit, revolutionizing social media advertising. It introduced detailed targeting options, allowing businesses to show ads based on demographics, interests, and even behaviors.

Real-Life Example: Small businesses thrived using PPC advertising. A local bakery, for instance, could run Facebook ads targeting users within a 5-mile radius who had an interest in desserts—something that was impossible with traditional advertising.

4. The Mobile Marketing Shift – 2010s

As smartphones became an essential part of everyday life, mobile marketing took center stage. **By 2016, mobile internet usage surpassed desktop usage for the first time.** Companies optimized their websites for mobile, developed apps, and started using SMS marketing and push notifications.

Google also introduced **Mobile-First Indexing**, prioritizing mobile-friendly websites in search rankings. Marketers had to rethink their strategies to ensure they provided seamless mobile experiences.

Real-Life Example: Domino's Pizza saw a **30% increase in online orders** after optimizing its app and launching a voice-ordering feature. This proved how critical mobile experiences were for modern consumers.

The Rise of AI & Automation in Marketing

Now, we are witnessing yet another massive shift—the rise of **Artificial Intelligence (AI) and automation in marketing.** AI has moved beyond being just a futuristic concept to becoming an **essential tool for optimizing marketing efforts, personalizing user experiences, and improving efficiency.**

1. AI-Powered Chatbots & Customer Engagement

Gone are the days when customer service was limited to phone calls and emails. AI-powered chatbots now provide **instant responses 24/7,** enhancing customer satisfaction.

Real-Life Example: Sephora's chatbot on Facebook Messenger offers personalized beauty recommendations based on user preferences. **This not only improves customer engagement but also drives sales by guiding users to the right products.**

2. Predictive Analytics & Data-Driven Decisions

AI tools can analyze **massive amounts of data in seconds** to predict consumer behavior. Companies can now determine **which marketing campaigns will be successful, what products customers are likely to buy next, and how to optimize ad spending.**

Real-Life Example: Netflix uses AI to analyze viewing habits and recommend personalized content. **This AI-driven strategy has contributed significantly to customer retention, with over 80% of content viewed coming from recommendations.**

3. Content Creation & Personalization

AI-powered tools like Jasper AI and Copy.ai help marketers generate blog posts, email subject lines, and even ad copies. AI is also enhancing personalization, ensuring every user gets content tailored to their interests.

Real-Life Example: Amazon's recommendation engine uses AI to suggest products based on past searches and purchases. **This level of personalization has helped Amazon achieve over 35% of its revenue from recommendations alone.**

4. Marketing Automation for Efficiency

AI-driven automation tools like HubSpot, Marketo, and ActiveCampaign help businesses streamline tasks like email marketing, lead nurturing, and social media posting.

Real-Life Example: A SaaS company using AI-driven email automation saw a **30% increase in conversion rates** by sending personalized follow-ups based on user behavior.

Conclusion: The Future is AI-Driven

Digital marketing has come a long way—from newspaper ads to hyper-targeted AI-driven campaigns. Today, businesses that embrace AI and automation are not just keeping up with trends—they're leading the way.

As we move forward, the integration of AI in digital marketing will only deepen. Businesses will continue to use predictive analytics, voice search optimization, and AI-generated content to **connect with consumers in more meaningful ways.**

In the next chapter, we'll explore **how to craft an AI-powered digital marketing strategy** that helps businesses thrive in this new era. Are you ready to unlock the true potential of AI in marketing? Let's dive in!

Chapter 2: Consumer Behavior in the Digital Age

Have you ever noticed how **the way we buy things today is completely different** from what it was a decade ago? I mean, think about it. There was a time when we relied on advertisements in newspapers, TV commercials, and radio jingles to tell us what was worth buying. We didn't have many options, nor did we question much about the brands we were purchasing from.

But today? The tables have turned. **Consumers, not businesses, control the market.** And if you're in the digital marketing space, let me tell you something—**if you don't keep up with this shift, your brand could disappear faster than you can say "algorithm update."**

Let's dive deep into **how consumer behavior has changed, why personalization matters more than ever, and how brands need to be careful with privacy and ethics in marketing.**

The Power Shift: How Consumers Control the Market

There's something incredibly powerful about the **internet and social media**—they have completely disrupted how businesses operate. In the past, brands dictated trends. They told people what was in fashion, what to eat, what to drive, and how to live. Consumers had little say.

Today? **The consumer has the final word.**

One bad review, one viral tweet, or one influencer calling out a brand, and **entire businesses can crumble overnight.**

Remember the **Pepsi ad with Kendall Jenner** that received massive backlash? The brand thought they were promoting peace and unity, but consumers saw it as tone-deaf. Within hours, it became one of the most criticized campaigns of all time, and Pepsi had to pull it down.

Or take the **power of influencer marketing**—one positive recommendation from a trusted creator can **skyrocket** a brand's sales. Just look at what happened when Elon Musk tweeted about Dogecoin—**the market exploded within hours.**

How Consumer Behavior Has Evolved

1. **Consumers Research Before They Buy**
   Today's customers won't just trust what brands say—they'll **Google it, watch reviews on YouTube, and check Twitter reactions** before making a decision.
2. **Social Proof Is the New Word-of-Mouth**
   Do you buy something without checking the reviews first? Most of us don't. Studies show **91% of consumers trust online reviews as much as personal recommendations.**
3. **Engagement Matters More Than Ads**
   People don't just want **to be sold to**—they want brands to talk to them, reply to their comments, and interact like humans. The brands that build relationships win.
4. **Loyalty Is No Longer Guaranteed**
   Unlike the past, where people stuck to brands for years, today's consumers **switch instantly** if they find a better offer, better service, or a brand that aligns more with their values.

The takeaway? **If you're not listening, engaging, and providing value, your brand will struggle.**

The Role of Personalization and Hyper-Targeting

Now, let's talk about something that **completely changed the game—personalization.**

Imagine this: You walk into your favorite coffee shop, and before you even place an order, the barista smiles and says, **"The usual?"** That **feeling of being known and understood** is what makes us **want to come back.**

That's exactly what consumers expect from brands today. **They don't want generic ads or one-size-fits-all marketing. They want experiences that feel tailor-made for them.**

Think about how **Netflix suggests the perfect shows based on your viewing history** or how Amazon **recommends products you didn't even know you needed but now desperately want.**

How Hyper-Targeting Works

1. **AI & Data Analytics Know Your Preferences**
   Ever searched for something on Google, and then suddenly, ads for that exact product start following you everywhere? That's AI-powered hyper-targeting in action.
2. **Content Is Tailored for YOU** The emails you receive, the ads you see, even the order in which content appears in your feed—it's all **strategically curated** based on your behavior.
3. **Retargeting Makes Sure You Don't Forget**
   Left something in your cart but didn't buy? **You'll soon see a reminder email or ad nudging you to complete the purchase.**

Real-Life Example: The Genius of Spotify Wrapped

Every year, Spotify does something brilliant—it gives **every user a completely personalized year-in-review called "Spotify Wrapped."**

It shows them:

◈ Their most-played songs

◈ Their top artists

◈ The total minutes they spent listening

And what happens? **Millions of people share it online, giving Spotify massive free marketing.**

This is the power of personalization—it doesn't just make users feel valued, it makes them feel **seen.**

If your brand isn't doing this, you're missing out on one of the biggest marketing opportunities of this digital era.

Privacy Concerns & Ethical Marketing

But here's the flip side—**where do we draw the line?**

Because while consumers love personalization, **they don't love the idea of brands tracking their every move.**

The Privacy Dilemma

1. **People Want Personalization, But They Fear Data Misuse**
   Studies show that while 83% of consumers want a personalized experience, **73% are worried about how their data is used.**
2. **Big Data Scandals Have Created Trust Issues**
   Remember the **Facebook-Cambridge Analytica** scandal? It shook the entire world and **made people extremely cautious about how their data is collected.**
3. **Laws Are Getting Stricter** Governments worldwide have introduced regulations like **GDPR in Europe** and **CCPA in California**, which force brands to be **transparent about data collection.**

How Brands Can Market Ethically

So, how can you **balance personalization and privacy?**

◇ **Be Transparent About Data Collection** Tell your users what data you're collecting and how it will benefit them.

◇ **Ask for Permission** Don't just assume consent—**make sure users opt in before tracking them.**

◇ **Give People Control Over Their Data** Let users **adjust privacy settings** or opt out of tracking if they wish.

◇ **Focus on Value, Not Just Sales** Ethical brands don't just push products—they **help, educate, and engage their audience** in a meaningful way.

Take Apple, for example. They've made **privacy a selling point,** constantly reminding users that **their data is safe and not sold to advertisers.**

This approach has **boosted consumer trust** and helped Apple **stand out in an era of increasing data concerns.**

Final Thoughts: The Future of Consumer Behavior

One thing is clear—**consumers will continue to shape the future of marketing.**

Brands that **listen, personalize, and respect privacy** will thrive. Those that ignore these changes? Well, they won't last long.

Marketing is no longer just about selling—it's about **building relationships.** It's about making people **feel heard, valued, and respected.**

So, as you move forward in the digital space, remember this: **Marketing isn't about your brand. It's about your customer.**

Master this, and you'll always stay ahead of the game. ◈

Chapter 3: The Role of AI in Digital Marketing

The Moment That Changed Everything

A few years ago, I had a conversation that completely changed my perspective on digital marketing.

I was sitting across from a marketing director of a well-known retail brand. He looked frustrated.

"Jayant, we've spent weeks crafting our marketing campaign, analyzing data, and predicting what customers want. And yet, we're struggling to get real engagement. The numbers are just... flat."

I leaned back in my chair, smiled, and asked, *"What if I told you that AI could do all of this for you—faster, smarter, and with better results?"*

His eyes widened.

"AI? You mean robots taking over marketing? Sounds like science fiction."

I laughed. *"Not science fiction—science reality. AI isn't replacing marketers; it's making them superhuman."*

And that's exactly what this chapter is about.

We're not just talking about technology. We're talking about a **fundamental shift**—how AI is transforming marketing strategies, **predicting customer behavior**, and creating **hyper-personalized experiences** that weren't possible before.

Let's dive in.

How AI is Transforming Marketing Strategies

The "Gut Feeling" vs. AI-Driven Decisions

For decades, marketers relied on **gut feelings, experience, and intuition** to make decisions.

Remember the old-school marketing approach?

◇ You create a campaign based on broad assumptions.

◇ You spend **weeks** analyzing trends and data.

◇ You cross your fingers and hope the audience responds.

But hope isn't a strategy.

Then came AI. And suddenly, businesses had the power to:

◇ **Analyze billions of data points in seconds.**

◇ **Predict trends before they happen.**

◇ **Deliver personalized experiences at scale.**

The Starbucks Story: AI Knows Your Coffee Better Than You Do

Imagine this. You wake up, grab your phone, and see a **personalized message from Starbucks**:

"Good morning! How about a Caramel Macchiato today? You usually grab one around this time. Here's 10% off your next order."

Sounds like magic, right?

It's not. It's AI.

◇ AI tracks **your past orders, location, and weather conditions.**

◇ It **predicts** what drink you might want.

◈ It sends you **the right offer at the right time.**

Now, instead of a **generic email blast**, Starbucks is having **a one-on-one conversation** with you—at scale.

◈ **Takeaway:** AI doesn't just automate marketing. **It makes it smarter, more personal, and more effective.**

Machine Learning, Predictive Analytics, and Chatbots

Predicting the Future: The Magic of Machine Learning

I remember sitting with a retail client who asked me:

"Jayant, how do companies like Amazon always seem to know what I want before I even search for it?"

The answer? **Machine Learning.**

Imagine you're running an online clothing store. A customer buys a pair of running shoes.

◈ AI **analyzes past purchases** and realizes that most people who buy these shoes also buy **running socks and water bottles** within a week.

◈ Before the customer even thinks about it, AI **suggests these items**, increasing sales **without feeling pushy.**

◈ This is why **Amazon's "Recommended for You" section drives nearly 35% of its sales.**

The Netflix Effect: How AI Knows Your Binge-Watching Habits

Ever wondered how Netflix **always** knows exactly what show you'll love next?

It's **not** luck. It's machine learning.

Netflix tracks:

◈ **What you watch**

◈ **How long you watch**

◈ **When you pause, rewind, or skip**

And then, like a **digital fortune teller,** it predicts what you'll want to watch next.

◈ **Takeaway:** AI doesn't just process data—it **turns it into predictive insights that drive engagement and sales.**

Chatbots: Your 24/7 Digital Salesperson

A few months ago, I ordered food online. I had a question about my order, so I went to the website's chat section.

Within **two seconds**, a chatbot responded:

"Hi Jayant! Your order is on its way and will arrive in 10 minutes. Need anything else?"

I was impressed.

Chatbots have changed the game.

◈ **Why Chatbots Are a Game-Changer:**

◈ **They respond instantly, 24/7** – No human agent needed.

◈ **They improve over time** – Learning from conversations, they get smarter.

◈ **They feel human** – Thanks to AI, they understand context and emotions.

⬦ Example: H&M's AI Stylist

- H&M's chatbot suggests **outfits based on your style preferences.**
- Customers love it because it feels like **a personal shopping assistant.**

⬦ **Takeaway:** AI-powered chatbots aren't just answering questions—they're **building customer relationships.**

AI-Powered Content Generation & Personalization

The $10 Million AI Blog Post

A few years ago, an AI-generated blog post went viral.

Why? Because it was **so well-written that no one knew it was AI.**

Brands like **Forbes, The Washington Post, and even Google** now use AI to:

⬦ **Generate high-quality content** in minutes.

⬦ **Optimize blog posts for SEO automatically.**

⬦ **Write product descriptions and social media posts.**

But does this mean **AI will replace human writers?**

Absolutely not.

AI can generate content, but it lacks the **creativity, storytelling, and emotional intelligence that humans bring.**

Hyper-Personalization: The Future of Marketing

Let's go back to the Starbucks story.

What if instead of **sending the same promotion to everyone,** Starbucks **only sent it to people who actually cared?**

That's what AI does.

◈ **Example: Spotify's AI-Driven Playlists**

- **Discover Weekly:** AI analyzes your music taste and **creates a playlist just for you.**
- **Daily Mix:** A mix of your favorites + new discoveries.

This is why **Spotify users stay engaged for hours.**

◈ **Takeaway:** People don't want more content. **They want relevant content. AI makes that happen.**

Final Thoughts: AI is Here to Stay

So, let's go back to my conversation with that marketing director.

A few months after our chat, he called me.

"Jayant, we did it. We integrated AI into our marketing, and the results? Insane. Our engagement is up 300%. Customers feel like we actually know them. And the best part? AI does all the heavy lifting."

That's the power of AI.

◈ **Brands that embrace AI will dominate.**

◈ **Brands that ignore it? They'll struggle.**

AI isn't about **robots taking over.** It's about **helping businesses become smarter, faster, and more personal than ever before.**

So the real question is...

Are you ready to leverage AI and take your marketing to the next level?

Because those who do?

They won't just survive. **They'll thrive.**

Chapter 4: Data-Driven Marketing Strategies

"We Have Too Much Data!" - The Problem That Led to a Revolution

A few years ago, I was sitting in a boardroom with a group of marketing executives from a well-known retail brand. The CMO sighed in frustration and said,

"Jayant, we have tons of data—customer demographics, purchase history, social media interactions—but we don't know how to use it effectively!"

I smiled because I had heard this story **so many times before**.

"So, you have all the fuel you need," I said, *"but no engine to turn it into power?"*

The team nodded.

This is the **modern marketing dilemma**—businesses have more data than ever before, but very few know how to **convert it into actionable insights** that drive revenue.

In this chapter, we're going to explore how businesses can **harness the power of data, use AI-driven tools, and create marketing strategies that are not just data-informed but data-powered.**

Importance of Data Analytics in Marketing

Data: The New Oil

If you've been in business long enough, you've probably heard the phrase:

"Data is the new oil."

But let's take this analogy further.

Imagine you have **barrels of crude oil** sitting in a warehouse. It's valuable, sure, but unless you refine it into **gasoline, diesel, or jet fuel**, it's **useless** for practical applications.

This is exactly how data works.

◈ **Fact:** By 2025, the world will generate **463 exabytes of data per day** (that's 1 billion gigabytes!).

Yet, a study by Forrester found that **60-73% of all enterprise data goes unused for analytics.**

Why? Because most businesses:

◈ Collect massive amounts of data but don't know what to do with it.

◈ Lack the right tools to analyze and extract insights.

◈ Don't integrate data into their decision-making process.

How Data Transformed Nike's Business Strategy

Let's talk about **Nike.**

Nike, once a traditional retail-driven brand, completely transformed itself by becoming **a data-driven company.**

◈ In 2018, they acquired **Zodiac**, a consumer analytics firm, to help predict customer behavior.

◈ They **tracked every digital interaction**—from what shoes people browsed to how long they spent on a product page.

◈ Using this data, they launched **Nike Membership**, a hyper-personalized program where customers get exclusive deals **based** on their past purchases, fitness habits, and even local weather conditions.

◇ **Result?** Nike's direct-to-consumer revenue jumped **from $6.6 billion in 2015 to $18.7 billion in 2022**—powered by data.

◇ **Takeaway:** Data is **not** just numbers on a spreadsheet. **It's a goldmine of insights waiting to be tapped.**

Using Big Data for Customer Insights

The Power of Predicting Customer Behavior

Imagine this scenario.

You walk into your favorite coffee shop. Before you even reach the counter, the barista smiles and says:

"Good morning, Jayant! Your usual espresso with almond milk? Or would you like to try our new caramel blend?"

Wouldn't that feel amazing?

Now, imagine **every brand you interact with** could anticipate your needs **before you even express them.**

That's what Big Data does.

◇ **Fact:** 91% of consumers say they are more likely to shop with brands that provide **relevant recommendations and personalized offers.**

Amazon's Secret Weapon: Data-Driven Personalization

Amazon is a **data giant.**

◇ Every time you **search, click, buy, or even hesitate on a product**, Amazon is collecting data.

◈ Its recommendation engine **drives 35% of its total sales.**

◈ AI analyzes purchase patterns and suggests **exactly what customers are most likely to buy next.**

◈ **Example:** If you buy a new camera, Amazon won't just recommend any accessories. It will show you:

◈ The **most frequently bought lens** with your exact camera model.

◈ A memory card that is **compatible** with your device.

◈ A camera bag based on **what other buyers with your preferences purchased.**

◈ **Takeaway: Customers don't want choices. They want the right choices.** AI and big data make this possible.

Segmenting Customers Like Never Before

Traditionally, marketers used **broad categories** like age, gender, and location to segment customers.

But Big Data allows **hyper-segmentation**, breaking audiences into **micro-groups** based on:

◈ **Shopping habits** (Do they buy impulsively or wait for discounts?)

◈ **Browsing behavior** (Do they spend time on high-end products or budget options?)

◈ **Engagement patterns** (Do they interact more with emails, social media, or push notifications?)

◈ **Example: Netflix's AI-Powered Viewer Segmentation**

Netflix **doesn't just categorize you** as a 'comedy lover' or 'action fan.' Instead, it creates hyper-personalized segments like:

◈ "Fans of dark humor comedies with strong female leads"

◈ "Viewers who binge-watch thriller series with surprise endings"

And then **curates content specifically for you.**

◈ **Takeaway:** The more personalized the experience, the higher the engagement.

AI-Driven Marketing Automation Tools

From Manual to Automated Marketing: A Game-Changer

For years, marketing was **manual**:

◈ Writing emails from scratch.

◈ Manually segmenting customer lists.

◈ Running ads based on guesswork.

But AI-driven automation changed everything.

◈ **Fact:** Businesses using AI-powered marketing automation **increase lead generation by 451%.**

Example: How Sephora Uses AI to Automate Marketing

◈ **AI-Powered Chatbots:** Sephora's chatbot, available on Facebook Messenger, provides **personalized makeup recommendations** based on a user's skin tone and preferences.

◈ **AI-Driven Email Campaigns:** Instead of sending generic newsletters, Sephora's AI analyzes past purchases and sends **tailored product suggestions** with limited-time offers.

◈ **Result?**

Sephora's chatbot **boosted engagement rates by 11%**, and their AI-driven email campaigns achieved **3x higher conversion rates**.

◈ **Takeaway:** AI doesn't just automate tasks—it **optimizes marketing to drive real business results**.

How You Can Implement AI-Driven Marketing Automation Today

◈ **Use AI for Email Personalization**

- Platforms like **HubSpot and Mailchimp** use AI to suggest subject lines that increase open rates.
- AI **automatically personalizes email content** based on customer behavior.

◈ **Leverage AI Chatbots for Customer Engagement**

- AI chatbots like **Drift and Intercom** handle 80% of routine customer inquiries **without human intervention.**
- AI-powered chat increases conversion rates by **40% or more.**

◈ **Run AI-Optimized Ad Campaigns**

- **Google Ads and Facebook Ads** use AI to optimize **targeting, bidding, and ad placements** in real time.
- AI-powered ads deliver **up to 50% lower customer acquisition costs.**

◈ **Takeaway:** AI-powered automation isn't just for big brands. **Every business—big or small—can use it to scale their marketing.**

Final Thoughts: Data-Driven Marketing is the Future

Going back to my conversation with the CMO, I remember what he said after I explained all of this:

"Jayant, I get it now. We don't just need data. We need to actually use it the right way."

And that's the key.

◇ **Brands that leverage data and AI will dominate.**

◇ **Brands that ignore it will struggle.**

The future belongs to those who can **turn data into actionable insights**—because in the digital world, **decisions made without data are just guesses.**

Are you ready to harness the power of data and AI in your marketing?

Because the businesses that do?

They won't just survive. They'll thrive.

Chapter 5: The Future of Search: AI & Voice Search Optimization

"Hey Google, How Do I Rank #1?" - The Changing Face of Search

A few months ago, I was sitting in a café, sipping my coffee, when I noticed something interesting. At one table, a young woman picked up her phone and said,

"Hey Siri, what's the best Italian restaurant near me?"

At the next table, a man in his 40s was manually typing on Google,

"Best Italian restaurants in Mumbai."

Both were looking for the same information, yet their approach was entirely different. This simple observation represents the transformation that search engines have undergone in recent years.

Some people still prefer typing and browsing through search results. Others want instant answers through voice commands. The way we search is evolving, and businesses that fail to adapt risk becoming invisible in this AI-driven digital landscape.

Let's explore how search engines have evolved, the growing influence of voice search, and how businesses can optimize for this new era.

The Evolution of SEO & AI's Role

SEO: From Keywords to Intelligence

Not too long ago, search engine optimization (SEO) was relatively straightforward. If you wanted to rank for the keyword **"best smartphones,"** all you had to do was:

- Stuff your webpage with the keyword "best smartphones" multiple times
- Acquire backlinks, even if they came from irrelevant websites
- Write generic content with little real value

But today, search engines have become much smarter.

Google no longer ranks pages based solely on keyword density. Instead, it evaluates **search intent.** AI now plays a crucial role in understanding context, user behavior, and engagement patterns.

Google's AI-powered algorithm, **RankBrain**, has been refining search results since 2015. This system processes **15 percent of new searches every day**—queries Google has never encountered before.

Let's consider an example.

Imagine a user searches for:

"Which smartphone should I buy for gaming under $500?"

Instead of just displaying pages that contain the phrase **"smartphone under $500,"** Google's AI will:

- Analyze millions of reviews, comparisons, and discussions
- Identify that the user is interested in gaming performance, not just price
- Show results featuring battery life, refresh rates, and processor speeds—even if they don't contain the exact words in the query

With **68 percent of online experiences beginning with a search engine,** AI is making sure that users find the most relevant content based on their needs, not just keyword matches.

This shift means that businesses must now focus on **delivering value-driven, high-quality content** rather than simply chasing keywords.

How Voice Search is Changing Search Engine Marketing

"Alexa, Find Me a Lawyer!" - The Rise of Voice Search

A decade ago, talking to machines seemed like science fiction. Today, it's an everyday reality.

Voice assistants like **Google Assistant, Siri, Alexa, and Cortana** process billions of searches every month. Consumers are rapidly shifting toward hands-free searches.

- **71 percent of consumers** now prefer voice search over typing
- By **2025, voice shopping is projected to reach $40 billion**
- More than **50 percent of adults use voice search daily**

How Voice Search Differs from Traditional Search

There are key differences between **typed and spoken** searches.

- **Typed Search:** "Best running shoes"
- **Voice Search:** "Hey Google, what are the best running shoes for marathon training?"

Voice searches are typically:

- **Longer and conversational**
- **Question-based**, using who, what, when, where, and how
- **Localized**, with 58 percent of voice searches focusing on local businesses

For example, if a customer says, **"Where is the nearest pharmacy?"**, Google prioritizes businesses that have optimized their **Google My Business** profiles with accurate location data and customer reviews.

With voice search growing rapidly, businesses must adapt to ensure they are part of this conversation.

How to Optimize for Voice Search

1. **Focus on Conversational Keywords**
   - Instead of targeting "best smartphones," optimize for "Which smartphone should I buy under $500?"
   - Think about how people **talk**, not just how they type
2. **Improve Local SEO**
   - Since **58 percent of voice searches are for local businesses**, ensure your **Google My Business listing** is up to date
   - Optimize for "near me" searches by including location-based keywords
3. **Structure Your Content for Questions**
   - Create FAQ pages that answer common voice search queries
   - Instead of "Top 10 Smartphones," write "What is the best smartphone under $500 for gaming?"
4. **Improve Site Speed**
   - **Voice search favors fast-loading websites**
   - Since **53 percent of users abandon sites** that take longer than three seconds to load, optimizing page speed is critical

If a business does not optimize for voice search, it risks being left behind in this AI-driven era of search.

Optimizing for Featured Snippets & AI-Driven Search

What Are Featured Snippets?

When you ask Google a question, you might notice that **the answer appears at the top of the search results, even before traditional rankings.**

This is called a **Featured Snippet.**

Featured snippets provide concise, relevant answers to users' questions without requiring them to click through multiple pages.

- **55 percent of voice search results come from Featured Snippets**
- Featured Snippets boost **credibility and click-through rates**
- They are often referred to as "position zero" in search rankings

How to Optimize for Featured Snippets

1. **Answer Questions Directly**
   - Google prefers **clear, concise answers**
   - Instead of lengthy explanations, provide **a 40-50 word response** to direct queries
2. **Use Lists and Bullet Points**
   - Google favors structured content
   - Example: Instead of writing, "The best gaming laptops have high refresh rates, strong GPUs, and great cooling systems," break it down into:
     - High refresh rates
     - Strong GPUs
     - Great cooling systems
3. **Format Content with Headings**
   - Break content into **H1, H2, and H3 headings** so

Google understands structure
- ○ Example: "What are the best digital marketing strategies?" should be a clear subheading
4. **Optimize for Mobile & Voice Search**
    - ○ Most Featured Snippets are voice search-friendly
    - ○ Ensure content is **easy to read, fast-loading, and mobile-optimized**

Winning a Featured Snippet means your content is not just ranking well—it is Google's chosen answer.

Final Thoughts: The Future of AI-Driven Search is Here

As I finished my coffee that day at the café, I reflected on how search has evolved.

The young woman using voice search and the man manually typing his query represented the two worlds we are transitioning between.

The future of search is no longer about **what we type**—it is about **how we ask.**

- Voice search is growing exponentially
- AI is reshaping SEO
- Businesses that adapt will thrive, while those that don't will disappear from search results

If you are still relying on traditional SEO tactics, you are already behind.

If you embrace AI-powered search, voice optimization, and structured content, you are preparing for the future of digital discovery.

The question is—are you ready for the future of search?

Because those who adapt will be the ones who lead.

Chapter 6: The Future of Social Media Marketing

"Scrolling Through the Future" – How AI is Redefining Social Media

It was a regular morning. I picked up my phone, opened Instagram, and started scrolling. Within seconds, I saw a post about AI-driven marketing strategies, an ad for a book on digital transformation, and a video recommending a café that happened to be right around the corner from my last meeting.

Coincidence? Not at all.

This is **AI in action.** Every time we scroll through our feeds, artificial intelligence is working behind the scenes, analyzing our interests, behaviors, and interactions to deliver content that keeps us engaged.

Social media has evolved far beyond just a place to share updates and photos. It is now **a highly sophisticated, AI-powered ecosystem** that influences consumer decisions, shapes brand narratives, and determines what content reaches which audience.

In this chapter, we'll explore how AI is redefining social media marketing, personalizing our feeds, and even creating **AI-generated influencers** who are reshaping brand collaborations.

The Role of AI in Social Media Algorithms

How Social Media Algorithms Have Changed Over the Years

A decade ago, social media platforms displayed posts in **chronological order**—the most recent posts appeared first. If a brand posted something at 8 a.m., and a user checked their feed at 10 a.m., they'd likely see the content.

But today, that's no longer the case. AI-driven algorithms **decide what appears on our feeds based on engagement, relevance, and personal behavior patterns.**

Consider how these platforms use AI:

- **Facebook:** Uses AI to prioritize posts with higher engagement and ranks content based on **meaningful interactions**
- **Instagram:** Uses **machine learning** to curate posts based on users' past likes, comments, and interactions
- **TikTok:** Uses AI-powered recommendation engines to track watch time, user interests, and replays to serve the most engaging content

How AI Predicts User Engagement

AI has transformed the way content is ranked. Platforms use **predictive analytics** to assess which posts a user is most likely to engage with.

Let's break this down:

1. **AI Analyzes Past Behavior** – It tracks every post you like, comment on, or share.
2. **AI Recognizes Patterns** – If you frequently watch digital marketing content, you'll see more of it.
3. **AI Prioritizes High-Engagement Content** – The more engagement a post gets, the more likely it is to be shown to others.

This explains why some posts go **viral within hours**, while others disappear without a trace. AI ensures that only the most **relevant and engaging** content reaches the audience.

What This Means for Brands

For businesses and marketers, this means **organic reach is no longer guaranteed.**

- **Only 5.2% of Facebook posts** from brands are seen by their followers
- **Instagram's algorithm prioritizes content that gets quick engagement**—if a post doesn't perform well within the first hour, it's unlikely to reach a wider audience
- **TikTok's AI-driven "For You Page" (FYP) can make a brand viral overnight** if the content aligns with audience interest

To succeed in social media marketing today, brands need to **create AI-friendly content**—posts that drive engagement quickly and align with audience preferences.

How AI Personalizes Social Media Feeds

Why Do You See Certain Ads and Posts?

Ever wondered why after searching for running shoes, your social media feed is suddenly filled with sneaker ads? That's AI-powered personalization at work.

Social media platforms use **deep learning algorithms** to track user behavior and serve hyper-targeted content. Here's how it happens:

1. **AI Tracks Your Interactions**
   - Every like, comment, share, and time spent on a post

is recorded.

2. **AI Identifies Your Interests**
   - If you watch multiple travel vlogs, AI assumes you're interested in travel content.

3. **AI Delivers Personalized Content**
   - Your feed starts showing more travel deals, hotel recommendations, and destination guides.

The Power of AI in Social Media Advertising

Brands are now leveraging AI to create **highly personalized advertising experiences.**

- **Chatbots on Facebook and Instagram** use AI to provide real-time customer support
- **Dynamic AI ads** change in real time based on user behavior
- **AI-driven social listening tools** track brand mentions and industry trends

Real-Life Example: How Netflix Uses AI for Personalization

Netflix isn't just a streaming platform; it's an **AI-driven recommendation powerhouse.**

- **80% of the content watched on Netflix is based on AI recommendations**
- Netflix's AI tracks every second of user interaction—what you watch, pause, and rewind—to suggest content you're most likely to enjoy
- The result? Users stay engaged, spend more time on the platform, and rarely run out of content

Social media platforms operate in a similar way. They want users to stay engaged for as long as possible, and AI ensures that happens by curating content that **feels tailor-made** for each user.

The Rise of AI-Generated Influencers

Who Are AI Influencers?

Imagine scrolling through Instagram and seeing a post from a fashion influencer. She looks real, she interacts with brands, and she has millions of followers. But here's the catch—she doesn't exist.

AI-generated influencers are virtual personalities created using artificial intelligence.

Meet **Lil Miquela**, an AI-powered influencer with over **2.5 million followers on Instagram.**

- She collaborates with major brands like **Calvin Klein and Prada**
- She posts lifestyle photos, interacts with followers, and even releases music
- Despite not being real, she generates millions of dollars in brand partnerships

Why Brands Are Turning to AI Influencers

1. **Cost-Effective Marketing** – Unlike human influencers, AI influencers don't charge high fees for brand collaborations.
2. **No Controversies** – Since AI influencers are controlled by brands, there are **no risks of scandals or PR nightmares.**
3. **24/7 Availability** – AI influencers can engage with audiences 24/7 without breaks.

Are AI Influencers the Future?

While human influencers will always play a role in social media marketing, AI-driven influencers are becoming a game-changer. Brands that adopt AI influencers early can **gain a competitive advantage** in this evolving landscape.

Final Thoughts: The AI Revolution in Social Media is Here

As I continued scrolling through my feed that morning, I realized something—social media **is no longer just about people connecting with people.**

It's about **AI curating experiences, predicting behaviors, and even creating digital personalities.**

- AI **determines what we see** on social media
- AI **personalizes content** based on our interactions
- AI **is even creating influencers** that compete with real people

For brands and marketers, the message is clear: **Adapt or fade into irrelevance.**

If businesses want to stay ahead in the AI-driven era of social media, they must:

◈ **Create AI-friendly content** that drives engagement quickly

◈ **Leverage AI-powered advertising** for hyper-targeted campaigns

◈ **Consider AI influencers** as a future-proof marketing strategy

The future of social media isn't coming—it's already here. The only question is, **are you ready to embrace it?**

Chapter 7: Influencer & Creator Economy in the Digital Age

From Stardom to Social Influence – The Evolution of Influence

I remember a time when brand endorsements were reserved for **big-name celebrities**. If a brand wanted visibility, they would sign a Bollywood star, a cricketer, or a Hollywood icon. The more famous the face, the better the sales.

But today, things have changed. **Trust is the new currency.**

Instead of looking up to celebrities on TV, consumers now rely on **influencers and creators** who feel more *real, relatable,* and *authentic.*

Consider this:

- **70% of teenagers trust influencers more than traditional celebrities.** (Source: MediaKix)
- **92% of consumers trust influencer recommendations over traditional ads.** (Source: Nielsen)

From YouTube creators and Instagram bloggers to TikTok dancers and LinkedIn thought leaders—**the influencer economy has exploded.**

In this chapter, we'll explore how influence has shifted from celebrities to **micro & nano-influencers**, how **AI is revolutionizing influencer marketing**, and what the **future of brand partnerships** looks like in an AI-driven world.

The Shift from Celebrity Endorsements to Micro & Nano-Influencers

Why Celebrities No Longer Dominate the Market

Once upon a time, brands like Pepsi, Nike, and L'Oréal would spend millions signing celebrities to endorse their products. The logic was simple: **A famous face = consumer trust = more sales.**

But today, social media has **democratized influence.** Consumers now seek:

✔ **Authenticity** – They want genuine opinions, not scripted ads.

✔ **Relatability** – They trust people who are like them.

✔ **Engagement** – They want two-way interactions, not one-sided promotions.

This shift has led to the rise of **micro and nano-influencers.**

Who Are Micro & Nano-Influencers?

Influencer Type	Follower Count	Engagement Rate	Example
Celebrity Influencers	1M+ followers	1-2%	Priyanka Chopra, Cristiano Ronaldo
Macro-Influencers	100K - 1M	2-5%	Popular YouTubers, Instagram Bloggers
Micro-Influencers	10K - 100K	5-8%	Niche content creators
Nano-Influencers	1K - 10K	8-15%	Local experts, community leaders

Surprisingly, brands are now **preferring micro and nano-influencers** over celebrities.

Why? The Power of Micro & Nano-Influencers

1. **Higher Engagement Rates**
   ◦ Micro-influencers **generate 60% more engagement** than

macro-influencers. (Source: HubSpot)

2. **Cost-Effective for Brands**
    - A celebrity might charge **$1 million per post**, while a micro-influencer charges between **$100 - $500** per post.

3. **Targeted Niche Audiences**
    - Instead of mass marketing, brands can now target **specific, engaged communities** (e.g., fitness, travel, finance, gaming).

Real-Life Example: The Power of Micro-Influencers in Action

A beauty brand called **Glossier** built a multi-million-dollar empire **without celebrity endorsements**.

- Instead, they focused on **real customers and micro-influencers** to spread the word.
- **90% of their revenue** came from peer-to-peer recommendations.
- Their marketing strategy? **Trust over fame.**

This proves that the future of influencer marketing **isn't about how many followers you have—it's about how engaged and loyal your audience is.**

AI in Influencer Discovery & Performance Measurement

The Challenge: Finding the Right Influencer

With millions of influencers online, how can brands find the perfect one?

- **How do you know if their followers are real?**
- **How do you measure their impact?**
- **How do you ensure a good return on investment (ROI)?**

This is where **AI is changing the game.**

How AI is Revolutionizing Influencer Marketing

1. AI-Powered Influencer Discovery

Gone are the days when brands would manually search for influencers. AI can now:

✔ **Analyze millions of profiles** within seconds.

✔ **Detect fake followers** and engagement rates.

✔ **Match brands with the perfect influencers** based on audience demographics.

Example: Platforms like **Heepsy, Upfluence, and Traackr** use AI to find influencers **who align with a brand's target audience.**

2. AI in Performance Measurement

After selecting an influencer, AI helps brands track:

- **Engagement metrics** (likes, comments, shares, reach)
- **Conversion rates** (how many followers buy the product)
- **Sentiment analysis** (is the audience reacting positively or negatively?)

Example: AI tools like **HypeAuditor** analyze influencer credibility and audience sentiment, helping brands avoid influencers with **fake engagement.**

3. Predicting Influencer Success with AI

AI can even **predict which influencers will perform best** by analyzing:

- ✔ Past engagement trends

- ✔ Audience authenticity

- ✔ Content virality potential

This means brands can **invest wisely** instead of blindly spending on big names.

Future of Brand Partnerships & AI-Powered Influencer Marketing

The Rise of AI-Generated Influencers

Just when we thought influencer marketing had peaked, **AI influencers arrived.**

Meet Lil Miquela:

- A **virtual influencer with 2.5M Instagram followers**
- Collaborated with **Prada, Calvin Klein, and Samsung**
- She **isn't real**, yet brands are paying her millions

Why are brands investing in AI influencers?

✔ **No scandals** – AI influencers don't have human flaws.

✔ **24/7 availability** – They can promote products anytime.

✔ **Customizable personas** – Brands can create influencers tailored to their needs.

Will AI Replace Human Influencers?

Not entirely. While AI influencers are gaining traction, **human connection still matters.**

- AI influencers are great for aesthetics and futuristic branding.

- But real influencers build **trust through genuine experiences.**

The Future of Brand Collaborations

With AI in the picture, brand partnerships will evolve into:

✔ **Personalized AI-driven sponsorships** – Brands will use AI to match influencers with hyper-relevant audiences.

✔ **Voice & Video AI Influencers** – AI-powered avatars and voices will take over YouTube, TikTok, and podcasts.

✔ **Blockchain-Based Influencer Contracts** – Smart contracts will ensure transparency and fair payments in influencer deals.

How Brands Can Stay Ahead

For businesses looking to **thrive in AI-powered influencer marketing,** here's what you need to do:

◈ **Focus on authenticity** – Consumers value real, raw, and relatable content.

◈ **Use AI for influencer discovery & tracking** – Don't rely on follower count alone.

◈ **Experiment with AI influencers** – Consider virtual personalities for futuristic branding.

Final Thoughts: The Future of Influence is Digital & Data-Driven

Influence is no longer about being a **movie star or a sports icon.**

Today, **everyday people**—micro & nano-influencers—are shaping consumer decisions.

- **AI is making influencer marketing smarter, more efficient, and highly data-driven.**
- **Brands that embrace AI-powered influencer strategies will win the marketing game.**

The question isn't whether influencer marketing will continue to evolve.

The real question is: Are you ready to evolve with it?

Chapter 8: Social Commerce & The Rise of AI-Powered E-Commerce

The Future of Shopping is Already Here

I remember a time when shopping meant a trip to a mall, walking store to store, trying out products, and waiting in long queues at the billing counter.

Fast forward to today, and **shopping has transformed into a digital-first experience.** With just a few taps on a smartphone, we can browse through thousands of products, try them virtually using **Augmented Reality (AR),** and even get AI-powered recommendations tailored to our preferences.

Online shopping isn't just about convenience anymore—it's about **experience, personalization, and real-time engagement.**

Consider this:

- **Social commerce is expected to grow 3X faster than traditional e-commerce, reaching $1.2 trillion by 2025.** (Source: Accenture)
- **AI-powered recommendation engines drive 35% of Amazon's total revenue.** (Source: McKinsey)
- **Livestream shopping in China alone generated over $500 billion in sales in 2023.** (Source: Bloomberg)

In this chapter, we'll explore how **AI is revolutionizing e-commerce,** the rise of **livestream shopping & AR-powered experiences,** and how **AI-driven recommendations are redefining the future of retail.**

How AI is Transforming Online Shopping Experiences

From Traditional E-Commerce to AI-First Commerce

In the early 2000s, e-commerce was **basic and transactional**—you searched for a product, clicked "buy," and waited for delivery.

Today, AI has completely **revolutionized how we shop** online.

Imagine this:

- **You open an app**, and AI curates a list of products based on your past preferences.
- **You chat with an AI assistant**, which suggests products based on your mood and style.
- **You virtually try on clothes** using AR before making a purchase.
- **Your order is processed in seconds**, and AI optimizes delivery logistics for same-day shipping.

This isn't a vision of the future—it's happening **right now.**

Key Ways AI is Reshaping Online Shopping

1. AI-Powered Chatbots & Virtual Shopping Assistants

Gone are the days of scrolling endlessly through product pages. **AI chatbots and virtual assistants** are now helping customers:

✔ **Find the right product** instantly

✔ **Get personalized recommendations** based on their needs

✔ **Receive 24/7 customer support** without human intervention

Example:

- Sephora's **AI-powered chatbot** analyzes customer preferences and recommends makeup products that match their skin tone.

- H&M's **AI stylist** suggests outfits based on weather conditions and past purchases.

Result? **Faster decision-making, fewer returns, and higher customer satisfaction.**

2. AI in Visual Search & Image Recognition

Have you ever seen a product you love but didn't know what it's called?

Thanks to **AI-powered visual search**, now you can just **upload a photo** and AI will find the closest match available online.

Example:

- Pinterest's **AI-driven Lens tool** allows users to take a photo of an item and find similar products to buy online.
- Google Lens enables users to search for outfits, home decor, and even books just by taking a picture.

This is a **game-changer for discovery-driven shopping** experiences.

3. AI-Powered Customer Reviews & Sentiment Analysis

With millions of products online, reading through hundreds of reviews can be overwhelming. AI solves this by:

✔ **Summarizing customer feedback** in simple, easy-to-read insights

✔ **Detecting fake reviews** using Natural Language Processing (NLP)

✔ **Analyzing sentiment trends** to help brands improve their products

Example:

- Amazon uses **AI to detect and remove fake reviews**, ensuring shoppers get genuine feedback.
- AI-driven sentiment analysis helps brands understand what customers love (or dislike) about their products.

Result? A **smarter shopping experience**, free from misinformation.

Livestream Shopping & Augmented Reality (AR) in E-Commerce

What is Livestream Shopping & Why is it Exploding?

Imagine a **QVC-style shopping channel** but in a digital, interactive format where consumers can:

✔ **Watch influencers & brand ambassadors showcase products**

✔ **Ask questions in real time**

✔ **Buy instantly with one click**

Livestream shopping **combines entertainment with instant purchasing**—a perfect blend for today's fast-moving consumers.

How Livestream Shopping is Transforming E-Commerce

- **China is leading the way**—livestream shopping generated **$500 billion in sales in 2023** (Source: Bloomberg).
- **In the US, TikTok, Instagram, and Amazon Live** have adopted livestream commerce, growing at a rapid pace.
- **Brands that use livestream shopping see a 10X higher conversion rate** than traditional e-commerce (Source: Shopify).

Real-Life Example: Livestream Shopping in Action

When Kim Kardashian launched her **SKIMS shapewear line** via livestream, she:

✔ Sold out thousands of products **within minutes**

✔ Engaged with millions of fans in real time

✔ Created a shopping experience that felt **exclusive & interactive**

This proves that **people don't just want to buy—they want an experience.**

Augmented Reality (AR) & Virtual Try-Ons

Another major innovation reshaping e-commerce is **Augmented Reality (AR).**

Problem:

- Online shopping **lacks the "try-before-you-buy" factor.**
- Customers often return products because they don't look as expected.

Solution: AR-Powered Shopping Experiences

✔ **Try on makeup & clothes virtually** (L'Oréal, Nike, H&M)

✔ **Preview furniture in your home** before purchasing (IKEA, Amazon)

✔ **See how accessories look on you** without stepping into a store (Ray-Ban, Warby Parker)

Example:

- L'Oréal's **AR-powered makeup app** lets customers try different shades before buying.

- IKEA's **AR feature allows users to place virtual furniture in their home.**

This reduces **return rates, improves customer satisfaction, and boosts sales.**

AI-Powered Recommendation Engines for Personalized Shopping

Why Personalization Matters in E-Commerce

Would you rather browse through **hundreds of random products** or have a store that **knows exactly what you want?**

AI-powered recommendation engines **make shopping feel personal.**

How AI Creates Personalized Shopping Experiences

1. Behavioral Tracking & Predictive Analytics

AI **analyzes past purchases, browsing history, and engagement patterns** to suggest highly relevant products.

Example:

- **Amazon's recommendation engine** contributes to **35% of its total revenue.**
- Netflix-style **AI-powered shopping suggestions** increase sales by **30-50%** for brands like Spotify and eBay.

2. Dynamic Pricing & AI-Driven Discounts

Have you ever noticed how **flight prices change** every time you check? That's **AI-powered dynamic pricing** at work.

✔ AI adjusts prices based on **demand, competition, and consumer behavior.**

✔ Brands like **Walmart & Amazon** use AI-driven pricing to stay competitive.

✔ AI offers **personalized discounts** based on user behavior, increasing conversions.

3. AI in Subscription-Based & Curated Shopping

AI-powered **subscription boxes** are now a massive trend.

Example:

- Stitch Fix uses AI to curate personalized fashion boxes for customers.
- Spotify recommends music playlists based on **listening habits.**

The result? **A hyper-personalized experience that keeps customers coming back.**

Final Thoughts: The Future of AI-Driven E-Commerce

The days of **static, one-size-fits-all shopping** are over.

Today, AI has made online shopping:

◇ **Personalized** (AI-driven recommendations)

◇ **Engaging** (Livestream shopping & AR try-ons)

◇ **Seamless** (AI-powered chatbots & dynamic pricing)

Brands that **leverage AI in e-commerce** will dominate the market, while those that resist change **risk falling behind.**

The question isn't whether AI will shape the future of shopping.

The real question is: Are you ready for the AI-powered retail revolution?

Chapter 9: AI in Paid Advertising & Performance Marketing

The Evolution of Advertising: From Manual to AI-Driven Precision

There was a time when running an ad meant **placing a billboard on a busy street** or **buying space in a newspaper.** Advertisers had little control over who saw their message, and success was measured in estimates rather than hard data.

Fast forward to today, and the game has completely changed. **AI is redefining paid advertising, making it smarter, faster, and incredibly precise.**

Imagine a world where:

✔ AI **automatically finds the perfect audience** for your product.

✔ AI **predicts which ad creative will perform best** before you even launch it.

✔ AI **optimizes your ad spend in real-time**, ensuring every dollar is maximized.

Sounds futuristic? **It's happening right now.**

Consider this:

- **Programmatic advertising now accounts for 90% of all digital display ad spending.** (Source: Statista)
- **AI-powered ad targeting can increase conversion rates by up to 50%.** (Source: Forbes)
- **Google's AI-driven Performance Max campaigns have**

helped brands achieve a **15% higher ROI on average.**
(Source: Google)

In this chapter, we'll explore how **AI is revolutionizing paid advertising, the future of Google, Meta, and TikTok ads, and how AI is reshaping ad creatives for better performance.**

Programmatic Advertising & AI-Driven Ad Targeting

The Old Way vs. The AI-Powered Way

Before AI, advertising was a **manual and time-consuming process:**

✔ Marketers had to **manually define their target audience.**

✔ Ad bidding was done through **guesswork and experience.**

✔ Performance tracking was **slow and reactive.**

AI has changed everything.

Today, programmatic advertising—powered by AI—**automatically buys and places ads in real-time, targeting the right audience at the right time with the right message.**

What is Programmatic Advertising?

Simply put, **programmatic advertising** uses AI to buy and place digital ads in milliseconds. It analyzes data **in real time** and determines which ads should be shown to which users, at what price, and on which platform.

How AI-Driven Ad Targeting Works

1. Audience Segmentation & Predictive Targeting

AI collects and analyzes **billions of data points** to identify customer behavior and preferences. It then segments audiences based on:

✔ **Demographics (age, location, gender, etc.)**

✔ **Online behavior (websites visited, time spent, etc.)**

✔ **Interests & purchase intent**

Example:

- **Amazon's AI-powered ads target users based on past purchases,** ensuring highly relevant product suggestions.
- **Netflix uses AI to personalize movie recommendations**—the same technology is applied to ad targeting.

2. Real-Time Bidding (RTB) & AI-Powered Ad Buying

Imagine AI acting as a **stock market trader for ads**—bidding on ad placements **in real-time** and ensuring your ads appear in front of the right audience at the lowest cost.

✔ AI **analyzes millions of ad placements** in milliseconds.

✔ It bids **only on the most valuable placements** based on user behavior.

✔ It **adjusts spending dynamically**, ensuring maximum ROI.

Example:

- **Google's Performance Max campaigns** use AI to optimize bids across YouTube, Display, Search, and Shopping ads.
- **Facebook's AI-powered Advantage+ campaigns** automatically adjust budgets for the best-performing ads.

3. Hyper-Personalization & Dynamic Ad Creatives

AI doesn't just **target users**—it **customizes the ad experience** based on their behavior.

✔ **Dynamic creatives** automatically adjust based on user interests.

✔ **AI-driven A/B testing** continuously refines ad elements (headlines, colors, CTAs, etc.).

Example:

- **Spotify uses AI to serve hyper-personalized audio ads** based on listening habits.
- **Nike's AI-powered display ads show different products** based on browsing history.

The result? **Higher engagement, better conversions, and lower ad costs.**

Future of Google Ads, Meta Ads, and TikTok Ads

1. The AI Revolution in Google Ads

Google Ads has **fully embraced AI** with features like:

✔ **Performance Max campaigns** (AI-driven ad placements across all Google properties).

✔ **Smart Bidding algorithms** (AI adjusts bids based on user intent).

✔ **Responsive Search Ads** (AI tests multiple headlines/descriptions to find the best combination).

The Future?

- AI will continue **reducing the need for manual campaign**

management.

- **Voice search & AI assistants** will shape ad formats.
- Google's **AI-generated ad creatives** will further optimize performance.

Example:

- **Google's AI-driven ad automation helped Samsung achieve a 17% increase in ad conversions** while reducing cost per acquisition.

2. Meta Ads: AI-Driven Social Media Advertising

With over **3 billion users,** Facebook & Instagram ads are **goldmines for businesses**—and AI is making them even more powerful.

✔ **Meta's AI Advantage+ campaigns** automate audience targeting and creative selection.

✔ **AI-driven Lookalike Audiences** help advertisers find new customers similar to existing ones.

✔ **Instagram's AI-powered visual recognition** ensures product ads appear to relevant users.

Future Trends:

- **Metaverse advertising** will use AI to place virtual product ads.
- **AI-powered interactive ads** will drive deeper engagement.
- **AI-generated influencer marketing ads** will replace traditional static ads.

Example:

- **Coca-Cola used Meta's AI-powered ad tools** to increase engagement by

30% with interactive Instagram Story ads.

3. The Rise of TikTok Ads & AI-Generated Video Content

TikTok's AI-driven algorithm is **one of the most powerful in the world**—and it's transforming digital advertising.

✔ **TikTok's AI recommends ads based on real-time engagement trends.**

✔ **AI-driven video editing tools** allow brands to create optimized content quickly.

✔ **AI-powered in-feed shoppable ads** turn views into instant sales.

Future Trends:

- AI will **auto-generate TikTok ad scripts** based on trending content.
- AI will enable **real-time facial expression tracking** for engagement-based ad placements.
- **Augmented Reality (AR) shopping ads** will create immersive brand experiences.

Example:

- **Guess used TikTok's AI-driven hashtag challenge ads**, leading to a 14.3% engagement rate and massive brand awareness.

The Role of AI in Ad Copy & Creative Optimization

1. AI-Generated Ad Copy: Writing That Sells

✔ AI analyzes **millions of high-performing ads** and **generates ad copy** based on proven success patterns.

✔ AI tools like **ChatGPT, Jasper, and Copy.ai** are revolutionizing ad creation.

✔ **Sentiment analysis ensures ad messaging aligns with audience emotions.**

Example:

- **eBay used AI-powered ad copy generation,** reducing cost-per-click (CPC) by 20%.

2. AI in Creative Optimization: The Art & Science of Winning Ads

✔ AI **automatically tests different ad visuals** to find the best-performing ones.

✔ AI-powered design tools like **Canva & Adobe Sensei** optimize ad creatives for engagement.

✔ **Neural networks analyze past performance** and predict which ad designs will convert best.

Example:

- **L'Oréal used AI to test 400 ad variations,** improving click-through rates by 35%.

Final Thoughts: AI is the Future of Advertising

Gone are the days when advertising was based on **intuition and guesswork.**

Today, AI is transforming advertising into a **data-driven, automated, and hyper-personalized experience.**

◇ **AI-driven targeting** ensures ads reach the right audience.

◈ **Programmatic advertising** makes ad buying real-time and cost-effective.

◈ **AI-powered creative tools** optimize ad copy & visuals for maximum impact.

The brands that **embrace AI in advertising** will lead the market. The ones that resist? **They'll struggle to keep up.**

The future of advertising isn't just digital—it's AI-powered.

Are you ready to leverage AI for your advertising success? ◈

Chapter 10: Growth Hacking Strategies for Digital Success

Introduction: The New Era of Growth Hacking

Imagine a startup with limited resources but a game-changing idea. They can't afford massive ad spends or celebrity endorsements, yet they grow from obscurity to millions of users within months. How? Through **growth hacking.**

Growth hacking is the art of using **creative, data-driven, and AI-powered strategies** to achieve exponential growth at minimal cost. It's not just for startups; even Fortune 500 companies use these tactics to stay ahead.

In this chapter, we will explore:

- How **AI is revolutionizing growth hacking**
- How **A/B testing & predictive analytics** maximize success
- How **AI-driven conversion rate optimization (CRO)** boosts revenue

Let's dive deep into **AI-powered growth hacking techniques.** ◈

AI-Powered Growth Hacking Techniques

1. AI-Driven Customer Insights & Behavior Prediction

Before hacking growth, you need to **understand your audience**—who they are, what they want, and how they behave.

Traditional Approach:

- Marketers relied on **surveys, website analytics, and intuition**

to segment customers.
- This process was **slow, reactive, and often inaccurate**.

AI-Powered Approach:

- AI analyzes **millions of data points in real-time**, identifying patterns in customer behavior.
- AI-powered tools like **Google Analytics 4, HubSpot, and Mixpanel** provide predictive insights.
- **Machine learning models** predict which leads are most likely to convert.

◈ **Example:** Amazon's AI predicts buying behavior with **90% accuracy**, recommending products before customers even think of them!

2. AI in Viral Marketing & Content Personalization

Going viral isn't luck—it's data science. AI helps brands create **personalized, shareable content** that resonates with the audience.

✔ **AI analyzes social media trends** and suggests content ideas. ✔ **AI-driven tools like ChatGPT & Jasper** generate engaging captions, blogs, and email copy. ✔ **Neural networks optimize video content** for platforms like YouTube and TikTok.

◈ **Example:**

- BuzzFeed used **AI-powered content generation** to boost engagement by **80%**.
- Netflix's AI-driven recommendation engine **increased watch time by 75%**.

3. AI in Email Marketing Automation

Email marketing has evolved **from mass blasts to hyper-personalized AI-driven communication.**

✔ AI **segments email lists automatically** based on user behavior. ✔ AI predicts **the best time to send emails** for higher open rates. ✔ AI-generated subject lines and content **increase click-through rates (CTR) by up to 50%.**

◈ Example:

- Spotify's AI-powered email recommendations increased **user engagement by 60%.**
- eBay used AI-powered email marketing, boosting **conversion rates by 31%.**

4. AI in Social Media Growth Hacking

Social media is the **playground of growth hackers**—and AI is their secret weapon.

✔ **AI-powered chatbots** (like ManyChat) increase engagement by **30%.** ✔ **AI-driven social listening tools** (Brandwatch, Sprout Social) track brand mentions in real time. ✔ **AI-generated hashtags and captions** optimize social media reach.

◈ Example:

- TikTok's AI-driven algorithm **increased user engagement by 100%** within two years.

5. AI-Powered Referral & Loyalty Programs

Referral marketing is one of the most **cost-effective growth hacks**—and AI makes it even better.

✔ AI identifies **high-value customers** and incentivizes them. ✔ AI **predicts the best referral offers** for different user segments. ✔ AI **optimizes reward structures** based on historical data.

◈ **Example:**

- Dropbox's AI-driven referral program **grew their user base by 3900% in 15 months.**

A/B Testing & Predictive Analytics

What is A/B Testing?

A/B testing is a **scientific approach** to growth hacking—comparing two versions of a webpage, email, or ad to see which one performs better.

Traditional A/B Testing vs. AI-Driven A/B Testing

Traditional A/B Testing	AI-Powered A/B Testing
Manual selection of variations	AI automatically generates & tests multiple variations
Time-consuming process	AI predicts outcomes in real-time
Limited data processing	AI analyzes billions of data points

◈ **Example:**

- Google uses **AI-powered A/B testing** to optimize ad copy, increasing click-through rates by **30%**.

How Predictive Analytics Enhances A/B Testing

✔ AI **predicts which version will win** before testing even starts. ✔ AI adjusts variations **dynamically in real-time.** ✔ AI-powered tools like **Optimizely and VWO** automate the entire process.

◈ **Example:**

- Booking.com uses AI-powered predictive A/B testing to **improve booking rates by 25%.**

Conversion Rate Optimization (CRO) with AI

Conversion Rate Optimization (CRO) is the **art of turning website visitors into paying customers.** AI is taking CRO to the next level.

1. AI-Powered Heatmaps & User Behavior Analysis

AI-powered heatmap tools like **Hotjar and Crazy Egg** track user behavior and identify friction points.

✔ AI detects **where users drop off** in the sales funnel. ✔ AI suggests design changes to **improve user experience (UX).** ✔ AI-powered chatbots **reduce bounce rates** by assisting users in real-time.

◈ **Example:**

- Airbnb used AI-driven CRO techniques to increase bookings by **15%.**

2. AI in Landing Page Optimization

AI analyzes landing pages **in real-time** and suggests improvements.

✔ AI **automatically tweaks layouts** for different audiences. ✔ AI predicts **which CTA buttons** will convert better. ✔ AI-powered A/B testing improves landing page performance.

◈ **Example:**

- Unbounce used AI-powered landing page optimization, increasing conversion rates by **31%**.

3. AI in Pricing Optimization

AI doesn't just **optimize marketing—it optimizes pricing.**

✔ AI analyzes competitor pricing **in real-time.** ✔ AI dynamically adjusts prices based on demand. ✔ AI predicts the **sweet spot for maximum conversions.**

◈ **Example:**

- Uber uses AI-powered dynamic pricing, increasing revenue by **30%**.

Final Thoughts: AI is the Ultimate Growth Hacker

Growth hacking has evolved from **intuition to intelligence**—and AI is the driving force.

◈ **AI helps businesses scale faster, at lower costs.**

◈ **AI-powered tools optimize every stage of the marketing funnel.**

◈ **AI predicts what works—before you even launch.**

Brands that **embrace AI in growth hacking** will dominate the market. Those that resist? **They'll struggle to compete.**

So, are you ready to supercharge your business growth with AI? ◈

Chapter 11: The Future of Content Marketing & Storytelling

The Evolution of Storytelling in the Digital Age

A few years ago, content marketing was all about blog posts, email newsletters, and social media updates. Marketers focused on crafting compelling messages to engage their audiences. Fast forward to today, and we are witnessing a revolution—AI-generated content, hyper-personalized storytelling, and immersive, interactive formats are reshaping the way brands communicate.

To truly understand this transformation, let's go on a journey into the future of content marketing, exploring how AI is bridging the gap between human creativity and machine efficiency, how video marketing is dominating digital spaces, and why interactive content is the next big frontier.

AI-Generated Content & Human Creativity: A Perfect Synergy

Imagine you're a content marketer for a growing e-commerce brand. Your team is swamped, struggling to create enough high-quality content to keep up with demand. Then, you introduce an AI-powered tool like Jasper or Copy.ai, and suddenly, blog posts, ad copy, and product descriptions are generated in minutes. It feels like magic.

But here's the real game-changer: AI doesn't replace human creativity—it amplifies it. **According to a report by HubSpot, 64% of marketers believe AI-generated content helps them scale their efforts without compromising quality.**

Let's break it down:

1. **Content at Scale:** AI tools can generate thousands of content

variations in seconds, making personalization at scale possible. For instance, Netflix uses AI to craft unique show descriptions tailored to each viewer's preferences.

2. **Idea Generation:** AI can analyze trends, past performances, and audience engagement to suggest relevant topics. Tools like BuzzSumo and ChatGPT help marketers brainstorm viral-worthy content.

3. **Content Optimization:** AI-driven tools like Grammarly and Hemingway App enhance readability, ensuring that content resonates with the intended audience.

4. **Real-Time Adjustments:** AI algorithms analyze user behavior in real-time, suggesting tweaks for better engagement. Platforms like Persado even optimize ad copy for emotional impact.

Yet, despite AI's impressive capabilities, **human creativity remains irreplaceable.** AI might generate the words, but humans infuse them with meaning, emotion, and cultural nuance. The best content marketing strategies will seamlessly blend AI efficiency with human storytelling.

Video Marketing & AI in Video Editing: The Era of Visual Storytelling

Did you know that 82% of all internet traffic comes from video content? According to Cisco, video has become the dominant form of digital communication, and AI is playing a massive role in making video marketing smarter and more effective.

Consider TikTok and Instagram Reels—two platforms thriving on short-form video content. The rise of AI-driven tools has made video editing accessible to everyone, not just professional videographers.

1. **AI-Powered Editing:** Tools like Runway ML and Descript

use AI to edit videos automatically, removing background noise, adding subtitles, and even generating video from text input.

2. **Automated Personalization:** AI helps tailor video content for specific audiences. Netflix's AI-driven thumbnails adjust dynamically based on what a user is likely to click.

3. **Deepfake & Virtual Influencers:** AI-generated avatars like Lil Miquela have millions of followers, proving that AI-driven characters can engage audiences as effectively as real influencers.

4. **AI-Driven Insights:** Platforms like YouTube Analytics use AI to predict which content will perform best based on viewer engagement patterns.

For brands, this means storytelling through video isn't just about creativity—it's about leveraging AI to optimize every frame for maximum engagement.

Interactive & Gamified Content Marketing: The Future of Engagement

Static content is fading. The new generation of consumers craves interaction. **According to Demand Gen Report, 93% of marketers believe interactive content is more effective at educating buyers than static content.**

Think about BuzzFeed quizzes, interactive infographics, or Nike's augmented reality (AR) sneaker try-ons—each one transforms passive users into active participants.

1. **Gamified Storytelling:** Duolingo, the language-learning app, has mastered this art. With leaderboards, badges, and streaks, it turns learning into a game, keeping users engaged for months.

2. **Augmented Reality Experiences:** Brands like IKEA use AR to allow customers to visualize furniture in their homes before purchasing, creating a seamless, immersive experience.
3. **AI-Powered Chatbots & Voice Assistants:** Conversational AI tools like ChatGPT or Google's Duplex simulate human-like conversations, making content consumption feel more natural.
4. **Live Polls & Surveys:** Platforms like Instagram Stories use interactive stickers, quizzes, and polls to engage audiences in real time, boosting engagement significantly.

This shift means that the future of content marketing will be **less about broadcasting messages and more about creating engaging experiences** that pull audiences in rather than pushing content at them.

What This Means for Marketers

So, what does all this mean for the future of digital marketing? The key takeaways are clear:

- **AI is your co-pilot, not your replacement.** Marketers who embrace AI for efficiency while retaining their creative intuition will thrive.
- **Video is no longer optional.** Brands must invest in AI-powered video marketing strategies to stay relevant.
- **Engagement is the new currency.** Interactive and gamified content is the future of digital storytelling.

The brands that win in this new era will be those that **balance data-driven insights with authentic, emotionally resonant storytelling.**

Final Thoughts: The Human Touch in an AI-Powered World

As much as AI is revolutionizing content marketing, the essence of storytelling remains deeply human. People crave connection, relatability, and authenticity—something that AI alone cannot fully replicate.

The future belongs to marketers who use AI to enhance creativity, not replace it. Imagine a world where AI assists in crafting personalized stories, but human intuition ensures that these stories inspire, entertain, and leave a lasting impact.

That's the future of content marketing, and it's already here.

Are you ready to embrace it?

Chapter 12: Ethical AI & Data Privacy in Marketing

The Fine Line Between Personalization & Privacy

In the world of digital marketing, personalization has become the gold standard. We, as marketers, strive to deliver tailored experiences, showing consumers exactly what they need before they even realize it. But here lies the paradox—how much personalization is too much? Have we crossed the fine line between offering value and intruding into people's lives?

Imagine this: You search for running shoes on one e-commerce site, and within minutes, ads for the same product flood your social media, email, and even YouTube recommendations. While some may find this convenient, others see it as invasive. This is the double-edged sword of AI-driven marketing.

A study by SmarterHQ found that 72% of consumers only engage with personalized marketing messages, yet 86% are concerned about data privacy. This signals a growing dilemma—how do we harness AI for better targeting while ensuring we don't alienate customers?

The answer lies in transparency and consent. Companies must focus on permission-based marketing, allowing users to opt in rather than unknowingly collecting data. Brands like Apple have already set the stage with their App Tracking Transparency (ATT) framework, forcing apps to explicitly ask users whether they want to be tracked. The results? A staggering 96% of U.S. users opted out of tracking.

So, the takeaway for marketers? Ethical AI marketing is not just about leveraging data but ensuring that consumers feel in control of their information. Brands that prioritize trust will win in the long run.

AI Bias & Ethical Concerns in Digital Marketing

AI is often perceived as a neutral, objective technology. But the truth is, AI inherits biases from the data it is trained on. If the dataset is flawed, the AI model will be too. This has led to significant ethical concerns in digital marketing, where biased algorithms can reinforce stereotypes and marginalize certain groups.

Take, for example, the case of facial recognition technology. Studies have shown that AI-powered facial recognition systems are less accurate for individuals with darker skin tones, leading to discriminatory outcomes. Now, think about AI in advertising. If an AI-powered marketing platform is trained on biased data, it may disproportionately favor certain demographics while ignoring others, creating a digital divide.

Consider this real-world scenario: In 2019, an investigation found that an AI-driven financial service offered lower credit limits to women compared to men, even when their credit scores were identical. This wasn't intentional discrimination, but rather, a case of biased training data. The same issue applies to marketing campaigns—AI may favor users based on historical engagement patterns, thereby excluding potential customers from diverse backgrounds.

To mitigate AI bias, businesses must:

- Audit AI algorithms regularly to identify and correct biases.
- Use diverse and representative datasets for training AI models.
- Ensure human oversight in AI decision-making.
- Make AI-driven marketing campaigns explainable and accountable.

Brands like IBM and Google have introduced AI ethics committees to ensure their algorithms align with ethical standards. This is a step in the right direction, but as AI continues to evolve, ethical considerations must remain a top priority.

Regulations Like GDPR, CCPA & the Future of Data Protection

In response to growing concerns around data privacy, governments worldwide have introduced strict regulations. The General Data Protection Regulation (GDPR) in Europe and the California Consumer Privacy Act (CCPA) in the U.S. have reshaped the way businesses collect, store, and use customer data.

Let's break it down:

- **GDPR (Europe):** Introduced in 2018, GDPR mandates that businesses obtain explicit user consent before collecting personal data. It also grants users the 'right to be forgotten,' meaning they can request data deletion at any time. Companies that fail to comply can face fines of up to 4% of their global revenue.
- **CCPA (California, USA):** This regulation allows consumers to know what personal data is being collected, request its deletion, and opt out of its sale. Unlike GDPR, CCPA is more focused on consumer rights rather than explicit consent.

So, what does this mean for digital marketers? It's no longer enough to simply collect and use data—we must do so responsibly, ensuring compliance with evolving regulations. Companies that fail to adapt will not only face legal repercussions but also risk losing consumer trust.

The Future of Data Protection in Marketing

Looking ahead, data privacy regulations will only become stricter. Countries like India, Brazil, and Canada are rolling out their own versions of GDPR. Meanwhile, third-party cookies—once a staple of digital advertising—are being phased out, with Google set to completely eliminate them by 2024.

What does this mean for marketers?

- The era of mass data collection is ending. First-party data (collected directly from customers) will become the most valuable asset.
- AI will play a bigger role in privacy-friendly marketing, leveraging techniques like Federated Learning to analyze data without storing it in centralized servers.
- Brands will need to prioritize ethical marketing strategies, ensuring transparency in data collection and usage.

One great example is Apple's approach to privacy. By implementing features like Mail Privacy Protection, which prevents marketers from tracking email open rates, Apple is reshaping digital marketing. While some marketers see this as a challenge, it also presents an opportunity to shift towards ethical, value-driven marketing.

Conclusion: The New Era of Ethical AI Marketing

The future of digital marketing isn't just about leveraging AI to boost conversions—it's about doing so responsibly. As marketers, we have a duty to ensure that AI is used ethically, data privacy is respected, and customer trust remains intact.

Companies that embrace ethical AI will not only future-proof their marketing strategies but also build long-term relationships with consumers. As the digital landscape evolves, the key to success lies in balancing personalization with privacy, mitigating AI bias, and staying ahead of regulatory changes.

The choice is clear: Ethical AI marketing isn't just a trend—it's the future.

Chapter 13: The Future of Work in Digital Marketing

How AI is Redefining Marketing Jobs & Skill Sets

The world of digital marketing is evolving at a breakneck pace, and artificial intelligence (AI) is at the heart of this transformation. If we rewind a decade, marketing was still largely driven by human intuition, creativity, and traditional tools. Today, AI has automated many aspects of marketing, from content creation to customer interactions, analytics, and ad placements. But does this mean that human marketers will become obsolete? Absolutely not. Instead, AI is redefining marketing jobs, shifting the focus from mundane tasks to strategy, creativity, and data-driven decision-making.

The Shift from Execution to Strategy

In the past, marketing teams would spend hours manually segmenting audiences, A/B testing ads, or analyzing website traffic. AI-powered tools like Google Analytics, HubSpot, and ChatGPT can now do much of this work in minutes. This has created a shift in job roles—marketers are no longer just executors of campaigns but strategic thinkers who interpret AI-generated insights to make informed decisions.

For instance, rather than spending hours setting up and optimizing Facebook Ads, marketers now focus on understanding consumer psychology and crafting compelling narratives while AI handles bidding and targeting in real time. Similarly, email marketing specialists are now leveraging AI-driven automation tools to personalize campaigns at scale, making data-backed decisions instead of manually sending out generic newsletters.

The Rise of AI-Augmented Creativity

AI is also augmenting creativity rather than replacing it. Tools like Jasper, Writesonic, and MidJourney assist in content generation, but they lack the emotional depth and originality of human creativity. A great example is Coca-Cola's AI-powered ad campaigns. The brand uses AI to generate insights and optimize placements, but human marketers still develop the brand's creative direction, storytelling, and emotional appeal.

So, the future isn't about AI replacing marketers—it's about marketers who know how to work alongside AI. The skill set required is shifting from pure execution to a combination of creative, analytical, and technical expertise.

The Need for Continuous Learning in the AI Era

If there's one thing that's certain about the future of digital marketing, it's that change is constant. The rapid adoption of AI means that marketers need to embrace lifelong learning to stay relevant. The skills that got someone a job five years ago may not be enough to secure one five years from now.

The Evolution of Skills in Digital Marketing

The traditional digital marketing skill set—SEO, PPC, content marketing, and social media management—has expanded to include data analysis, AI tools proficiency, and automation expertise. Marketers must now understand how AI-driven recommendation engines work, how to train chatbots to deliver personalized responses, and how predictive analytics can enhance user engagement.

A real-world example is how Netflix's recommendation algorithm works. While the algorithm does the heavy lifting, marketers must understand how to influence content strategies based on data patterns.

If you're in e-commerce, AI-driven product recommendations (like those used by Amazon) require marketers to understand consumer behavior, segmentation, and conversion strategies to fine-tune campaigns.

How Marketers Can Stay Ahead

- **Learn AI Tools**: Familiarize yourself with AI marketing tools like HubSpot, Marketo, and ChatGPT.
- **Develop Analytical Skills**: Data is the backbone of AI-driven marketing. Courses in data science and analytics can provide an edge.
- **Enhance Creativity**: AI can automate tasks, but storytelling and emotional intelligence remain human strengths.
- **Network and Collaborate**: The future of marketing involves collaboration between AI specialists, data analysts, and creative professionals.
- **Adaptability is Key**: Marketers who are willing to embrace new technologies will thrive, while those who resist change will struggle.

Opportunities & Challenges for Marketers in the Future

As AI continues to reshape digital marketing, new opportunities and challenges emerge. Marketers who understand how to leverage AI will find themselves in high demand, while those who ignore it risk becoming obsolete.

Opportunities in AI-Driven Marketing

1. **Hyper-Personalization at Scale**
   - AI enables businesses to deliver highly personalized marketing messages based on real-time data. A great

example is Spotify's AI-driven playlists, which curate music based on user behavior. Marketers who master AI-driven personalization will create more impactful campaigns.

2. **AI-Powered Content Creation**
   - While AI-generated content is becoming common, human creativity is still necessary for storytelling. Marketers who know how to blend AI-generated insights with compelling narratives will excel.

3. **Predictive Analytics for Decision-Making**
   - AI can analyze customer behavior and predict future trends. For example, Amazon's predictive analytics engine recommends products before users even realize they need them. Marketers can use such insights to stay ahead of consumer demands.

4. **Conversational Marketing & AI Chatbots**
   - Chatbots like Drift and Intercom are revolutionizing customer engagement. Companies that integrate AI chatbots into their marketing strategy are seeing higher conversion rates and improved customer satisfaction.

Challenges Marketers Will Face

1. **Job Displacement & Reskilling**
   - As AI automates routine tasks, some marketing roles may become redundant. However, this doesn't mean job losses—it means job evolution. Marketers must upskill and adapt to new AI-driven roles.

2. **Data Privacy & Ethical Concerns**
   - With the rise of AI comes greater scrutiny of data collection and privacy. Regulations like GDPR and CCPA require marketers to be more transparent

about how they use customer data.

3. **Over-Reliance on AI**
   ○ While AI can optimize marketing efforts, over-reliance on automation without human oversight can backfire. An example is when AI-generated ad placements go wrong, as seen with YouTube's brand safety crisis, where ads appeared alongside inappropriate content.

4. **Keeping Up with Rapid Technological Changes**
   ○ The pace of AI advancements means marketers must be agile. Learning doesn't stop once a new tool is adopted—constant experimentation and adaptation are necessary.

Conclusion: The Marketers Who Will Thrive

The future of work in digital marketing is exciting, challenging, and filled with opportunities. AI is not here to replace marketers; it's here to make them more efficient, creative, and strategic. The ones who will thrive are those who:

- Embrace AI as an ally, not a threat.
- Continuously learn and adapt to new technologies.
- Focus on human creativity and emotional intelligence, skills that AI cannot replicate.
- Understand data-driven decision-making and AI-powered analytics.

The marketers of tomorrow will be AI-powered strategists, blending data, creativity, and technology to craft compelling brand narratives and drive business growth. The future isn't about choosing between AI and human marketers—it's about leveraging both to create marketing strategies that are more effective, personalized, and impactful than ever before.

Chapter 14: Building Your Digital Marketing Strategy for 2030 & Beyond

Adapting to AI-Driven Digital Trends

The future of digital marketing is not just about staying relevant; it's about staying ahead. With AI and automation becoming integral parts of marketing strategies, businesses and marketers must adapt swiftly to the changing landscape. Imagine waking up in 2030 and realizing that traditional digital marketing methods are now obsolete. The way brands engage with customers has shifted dramatically—AI-driven tools handle real-time personalization, predictive analytics dictate marketing decisions, and immersive technologies like AR and VR redefine user experiences. This is not science fiction; it is the reality we are stepping into.

The AI Revolution in Marketing

By 2030, AI will not only power search engines, recommendation algorithms, and automated content creation but will also shape customer relationships through hyper-personalized experiences. Brands that fail to integrate AI into their marketing strategies will struggle to compete. A report by McKinsey states that companies leveraging AI in marketing can increase revenue by up to 30% while reducing costs by 20%. These figures highlight the transformative power of AI-driven digital trends.

Take Netflix, for example. The company's recommendation engine, powered by AI and machine learning, accounts for over 80% of the content streamed on its platform. This level of personalization will become standard across all industries. Businesses must prepare to integrate AI-powered chatbots, predictive analytics, and automated marketing campaigns to enhance user engagement and drive growth.

The Rise of Immersive Technologies

Another critical trend that will define digital marketing in the next decade is the rise of immersive technologies. Virtual Reality (VR), Augmented Reality (AR), and Mixed Reality (MR) are already transforming how brands interact with consumers. IKEA, for instance, uses AR to allow customers to visualize furniture in their homes before making a purchase. This level of interactivity will soon become the norm.

By 2030, we can expect AI-driven virtual influencers, 3D product try-ons, and interactive AI-generated content to dominate the digital landscape. Brands that embrace these trends early will gain a competitive edge in customer engagement and conversion rates.

How to Future-Proof Your Marketing Career or Business

The question every marketer and business owner must ask themselves today is: How do I prepare for the future of marketing?

1. Continuous Learning and Skill Development

AI and automation will redefine job roles in digital marketing, making continuous learning essential. According to the World Economic Forum, by 2025, 50% of all employees will need reskilling due to automation. This number will only grow as we approach 2030. Marketers must invest in upskilling themselves in AI, data analytics, machine learning, and emerging digital marketing technologies.

For example, learning how to use AI-powered tools like Jasper for content creation or HubSpot's AI-driven CRM will be crucial for staying competitive. Additionally, understanding coding languages like Python and SQL will give marketers an edge in data-driven decision-making.

2. Building a Data-First Mindset

In the AI era, data is the foundation of every successful marketing strategy. Companies that use data-driven marketing are six times more likely to be profitable year-over-year. Marketers must develop a deep understanding of consumer data, leveraging AI to analyze trends, predict customer behavior, and optimize marketing campaigns.

Google's AI-driven analytics tools, such as Google Analytics 4 and Looker Studio, offer businesses actionable insights into customer interactions. By mastering these tools, marketers can make informed decisions that drive growth.

3. Humanizing AI-Generated Content

While AI will take over many aspects of content creation, human creativity will remain irreplaceable. AI can generate articles, social media posts, and even video scripts, but it lacks the emotional depth that resonates with audiences. The key to success in 2030 will be blending AI efficiency with human storytelling.

A great example of this is Coca-Cola's AI-powered marketing campaigns. The company uses AI to analyze consumer preferences but relies on human creativity to craft compelling brand narratives. This combination ensures that AI-driven content remains engaging and authentic.

4. Mastering Omnichannel Marketing

The future of digital marketing will be omnichannel, seamlessly integrating online and offline experiences. Consumers will expect brands to provide a consistent experience across websites, social media, mobile apps, and even physical stores.

For instance, Starbucks uses AI-powered personalization across its app, website, and in-store experience. By analyzing purchase history and preferences, the company delivers customized recommendations and promotions, increasing customer loyalty and revenue.

5. Ethical AI and Privacy-First Marketing

With AI's growing influence, ethical considerations will become a top priority. Regulations such as GDPR and CCPA have already set the stage for stricter data privacy laws. By 2030, businesses that fail to prioritize ethical AI practices will face severe consequences, both legally and in terms of consumer trust.

Apple's recent privacy updates, which give users more control over their data, have reshaped digital advertising. Marketers must adapt to privacy-first marketing strategies, focusing on transparent data collection and ethical AI usage to build long-term trust with their audience.

Final Thoughts & Key Takeaways

As we approach 2030, digital marketing will be more dynamic, data-driven, and AI-powered than ever before. Businesses and marketers who embrace these changes with a proactive mindset will not only survive but thrive in this new landscape.

Here are the key takeaways to future-proof your digital marketing strategy:

- **Embrace AI and Automation** – Leverage AI-powered tools to enhance marketing efficiency, personalization, and predictive analytics.
- **Invest in Continuous Learning** – Stay ahead of emerging trends by upskilling in AI, data analytics, and omnichannel

marketing.

- **Focus on Data-Driven Decision Making** – Use AI-powered analytics to gain deep consumer insights and optimize campaigns.
- **Balance AI with Human Creativity** – AI can automate content creation, but human storytelling will remain essential for engagement.
- **Prioritize Ethical AI and Privacy** – Transparency and ethical AI usage will be critical in building consumer trust and complying with future regulations.
- **Prepare for Immersive Marketing** – AR, VR, and AI-generated influencers will redefine how brands interact with customers.

The next decade will be a golden era for digital marketing innovation. By preparing today, you can position yourself and your business for long-term success in the AI-driven marketing landscape of 2030 and beyond.

Conclusion

As we stand on the brink of a digital revolution powered by artificial intelligence, automation, and hyper-personalization, one thing is certain—**the future of digital marketing will not be defined by technology alone, but by those who learn to embrace and leverage it effectively.**

Reflecting on the Journey

When we embarked on this exploration of AI-driven digital marketing, the landscape appeared dynamic yet complex. We started by understanding how AI is fundamentally reshaping marketing—from automating mundane tasks to personalizing customer interactions at an unprecedented scale. We then delved into the **power of AI tools,** the **changing skill sets required for marketers,** and how businesses can stay ahead in an era where customer experience is king.

Looking back at history, every technological leap—from the printing press to the internet—has created winners and losers. Those who resisted change struggled, while those who adapted thrived. **AI in digital marketing is no different. It is not here to replace marketers but to empower them.**

The Mindset Shift: AI as an Opportunity, Not a Threat

The biggest lesson from this journey is that AI should not be feared but embraced. Imagine a marketing world where campaigns no longer rely on intuition alone but are backed by **real-time insights, predictive analytics, and deep customer understanding.** Instead of spending hours manually analyzing data, AI enables marketers to focus on what truly matters—**creativity, strategy, and human connection.**

For instance, consider brands that have successfully adopted AI-driven personalization. Netflix, Amazon, and Spotify don't just sell products or services; they craft **experiences tailored uniquely to each user.** These companies are not just leveraging AI; they are **reshaping customer expectations**—an expectation that every brand must now meet.

Key Takeaways for the Future

1. AI is Here to Stay—Adopt or Be Left Behind

Change is inevitable. Marketers and businesses who fail to embrace AI-driven strategies risk being overshadowed by those who do. The time to experiment with AI tools is **now**, not five years from now when your competitors have already mastered them.

2. Customer-Centricity is the New Rulebook

Consumers today demand **seamless, personalized, and engaging experiences.** If businesses don't provide them, someone else will. AI gives us the ability to understand customers at an intimate level, **predict their needs, and deliver hyper-personalized experiences.**

3. Continuous Learning is Non-Negotiable

The rapid evolution of AI and digital marketing means that what works today may be obsolete tomorrow. To stay ahead, marketers must commit to **lifelong learning.** Whether it's upskilling in AI tools, understanding data-driven storytelling, or mastering automation platforms, **stagnation is not an option.**

4. Ethics and Responsible AI Matter More Than Ever

With great power comes great responsibility. AI-driven marketing should be used to **enhance customer trust, not exploit it.**

Transparency, data privacy, and ethical AI implementation should be at the core of every strategy.

5. Creativity Will Always Be Irreplaceable

While AI can analyze, automate, and optimize, it cannot replace **human creativity, emotion, and storytelling.** The best marketing campaigns will always be those that **touch hearts, inspire action, and forge genuine connections.** AI is just the tool—**the human touch remains the magic ingredient.**

Final Words: The Future is Yours to Shape

As you step into the future of digital marketing, remember this: **technology is only as powerful as the hands that wield it.** AI is not about taking jobs but about redefining them. It is not about replacing creativity but about **amplifying it.**

Whether you're a seasoned marketer, an aspiring entrepreneur, or a business leader, the opportunity before you is immense. The digital marketing landscape of 2030 and beyond will be shaped by **bold innovators, curious learners, and strategic thinkers.**

The question is: **Will you be one of them?**

The journey doesn't end here. It's just the beginning of a new era—one where those who embrace AI, adapt to change, and stay ahead of the curve will lead the future.

The time to act is now. **Go forth and redefine digital marketing!** ◈

References

1. **How WSJ Readers Use AI at Work**
   https://www.wsj.com/tech/ai/ai-at-work-readers-59e23819
2. **Google Super Bowl Ad Gets Embarrassing Attention Before Game Even Happens**
   https://www.sfgate.com/tech/article/google-super-bowl-ad-edit-gemini-ai-20149836.php
3. **How Canada's Shopify is Weaving AI 'Magic' to Pull in Merchants**
   https://www.reuters.com/technology/artificial-intelligence/how-canadas-shopify-is-weaving-ai-magic-pull-merchants-2025-02-10
4. **Super Bowl Ad Results: AI Can't Compete With Sentimental Stories**
   https://www.wsj.com/articles/super-bowl-ad-results-ai-cant-compete-with-sentimental-stories-99b4a549
5. **AI in Marketing Statistics: How Marketers Use AI in 2025**
   https://www.surveymonkey.com/mp/ai-marketing-statistics
6. **AI and Marketing: What the Stats Show**
   https://martech.org/ai-and-marketing-what-the-stats-show
7. **5 AI Case Studies in Marketing**
   https://www.vktr.com/ai-disruption/5-ai-case-studies-in-marketing
8. **Artificial Intelligence (AI) Use in Marketing - Statistics & Facts**
   https://www.statista.com/topics/5017/ai-use-in-marketing
9. **10 Creative AI in Marketing Examples and Use Cases**
   https://www.mailmodo.com/guides/ai-in-marketing-examples
10. **70+ AI Marketing Statistics for 2024**

https://www.sixthcitymarketing.com/ai-marketing-stats

11. **AI Marketing Tools: Case Studies and Success Stories**
https://www.contentgrip.com/ai-marketing-tools-case-studies-success-stories

12. **154 Eye-Opening AI Statistics of 2024**
https://www.synthesia.io/post/ai-statistics

13. **AI in Marketing | Retail AI Case Study**
https://www.accenture.com/us-en/case-studies/artificial-intelligence/using-ai-improve-marketing-spend

14. **AI in Marketing Revenue Worldwide 2020-2028**
https://www.statista.com/statistics/1293758/ai-marketing-revenue-worldwide

15. **3 Best Case Studies of AI in Digital Marketing Campaigns**
https://cr8consultancy.com/3-best-case-studies-of-ai-in-digital-marketing-campaigns

16. **Artificial Intelligence (AI) Marketing Benchmark Report**
https://influencermarketinghub.com/ai-marketing-benchmark-report

17. **Leveraging Artificial Intelligence in Marketing: A Case Study Analysis**
https://www.gims.net.in/pdf/research/leveraging-artifivial-intelligence-in-marketing-a-case-study-analysis.pdf

18. **32 Essential AI Statistics You Need to Know in 2025**
https://thesocialshepherd.com/blog/ai-statistics

19. **Blog | Case Studies**
https://www.marketingaiinstitute.com/blog/tag/case-studies

20. **10 Amazing Statistics From The World of AI Marketing**
https://medium.com/%40dplayer/10-amazing-statistics-from-the-world-of-ai-marketing-d203df538b8e

21. **6 Key Applications of AI in Digital Marketing—Plus Case Studies, Challenges, and Future Trends**
https://www.agilitypr.com/pr-news/public-relations/6-key-

applications-of-ai-in-digital-marketing-plus-case-studies-
challenges-and-future-trends

22. **50+ Artificial Intelligence Statistics for Marketers in 2025**
    https://www.webfx.com/blog/marketing/ai-statistics

23. **Brands Using AI for Marketing: 6 Successful Case Studies**
    https://www.ai-scaleup.com/articles/ai-case-studies/brands-
    using-ai-for-marketing

Glossary of Terms

A

- **AI (Artificial Intelligence):** The simulation of human intelligence in machines, enabling them to perform tasks like learning, reasoning, and problem-solving.
- **A/B Testing:** A method of comparing two versions of a webpage, email, or ad to determine which performs better.
- **Algorithm:** A set of rules or calculations that AI and search engines use to process data and deliver results.
- **Augmented Reality (AR):** Technology that overlays digital elements onto the real world through devices like smartphones and AR glasses.
- **Automation:** The use of AI-powered tools to execute repetitive marketing tasks like email campaigns, chatbots, and social media scheduling.

B

- **Big Data:** Large volumes of structured and unstructured data that businesses analyze to identify trends and make decisions.
- **Bots:** AI-driven programs that simulate human interactions in customer support, social media, and marketing.
- **Bounce Rate:** The percentage of website visitors who leave without engaging further.

C

- **Chatbot:** AI-powered virtual assistants that simulate human conversations to answer customer queries.

- **Click-Through Rate (CTR):** The percentage of users who click on a specific link or ad compared to total views.
- **Content Personalization:** AI-driven customization of content based on user behavior, preferences, and demographics.
- **Conversion Rate Optimization (CRO):** The process of increasing the percentage of users who complete a desired action on a website.
- **Customer Data Platform (CDP):** A system that collects, integrates, and manages customer data from multiple sources.

D

- **Deep Learning:** A subset of machine learning that mimics the human brain to process complex data.
- **Digital Twin:** A virtual model of a physical object or system, used in AI-driven marketing simulations.
- **Dynamic Content:** Personalized website or email content that adapts based on user behavior.

E

- **Edge AI:** AI that processes data on local devices rather than relying on cloud computing.
- **Engagement Rate:** A measure of audience interaction, including likes, shares, and comments.

F

- **Funnel (Marketing Funnel):** The journey a customer takes from awareness to conversion.

G

- **Generative AI:** AI models capable of creating content, images, videos, and text.
- **Geo-Targeting:** Delivering content or ads based on a user's geographic location.

H

- **Hyper-Personalization:** AI-driven real-time customization of content and marketing messages based on individual behavior and data.

I

- **Intent-Based Marketing:** Targeting users based on their online activity and inferred intent.
- **Influencer Marketing:** Partnering with social media influencers to promote brands.

J

- **Journey Mapping:** Visualizing a customer's experience across touchpoints to improve marketing strategies.

K

- **Keyword Research:** Identifying terms people use in search engines to optimize content for SEO.

L

- **Lead Scoring:** Using AI to rank leads based on the likelihood of conversion.
- **Lookalike Audiences:** AI-driven audience modeling to target users similar to existing customers.

M

- **Machine Learning (ML):** A subset of AI that allows systems to learn from data and improve over time.
- **Marketing Automation:** AI-powered tools that streamline and automate marketing activities.

N

- **Natural Language Processing (NLP):** AI's ability to understand and generate human language.
- **Neuromarketing:** The study of consumer brain responses to marketing stimuli.

O

- **Omnichannel Marketing:** A seamless customer experience across multiple marketing channels.

P

- **Predictive Analytics:** AI-driven forecasting of future trends based on historical data.
- **Programmatic Advertising:** Automated, AI-driven digital ad buying.

Q

- **Quality Score:** A Google Ads metric that affects ad rankings and costs.

R

- **Retargeting:** AI-driven ad strategy to re-engage users who visited a website but didn't convert.

- **ROI (Return on Investment):** A measure of profitability in marketing campaigns.

S

- **SEO (Search Engine Optimization):** Strategies to improve website rankings in search engines.
- **Sentiment Analysis:** AI analyzing social media and online content to determine public sentiment.

T

- **Tokenization:** The process AI uses to break text into smaller units for analysis.
- **Touchpoints:** Customer interactions with a brand across different channels.

U

- **User Experience (UX):** The overall experience a customer has with a brand's digital presence.

V

- **Voice Search Optimization:** Adapting content for AI-driven voice assistants like Alexa and Google Assistant.
- **Virtual Reality (VR):** Immersive digital environments used in marketing.

W

- **Web Scraping:** AI extracting and analyzing online data for insights.

X, Y, Z

- **Zero-Party Data:** Data that users willingly share with brands for personalized experiences.
- **Zettabyte Era:** The current digital landscape where data generation exceeds trillions of gigabytes.

List of AI-Powered Marketing Tools & Platforms

Content Creation & Copywriting

1. **ChatGPT** – https://openai.com/chatgpt
2. **Jasper AI** – https://www.jasper.ai
3. **Copy.ai** – https://www.copy.ai
4. **Writesonic** – https://www.writesonic.com

SEO & Search Optimization

1. **Surfer SEO** – https://surferseo.com
2. **SEMrush** – https://www.semrush.com
3. **Ahrefs** – https://ahrefs.com

AI-Powered Video & Image Editing

1. **Synthesia** – https://www.synthesia.io
2. **Runway ML** – https://runwayml.com
3. **Canva AI** – https://www.canva.com

Chatbots & Customer Support

1. **Drift** – https://www.drift.com
2. **ManyChat** – https://manychat.com
3. **Tidio AI** – https://www.tidio.com

AI-Powered Advertising & Marketing Automation

1. **Persado** – https://www.persado.com
2. **Albert AI** – https://albert.ai

3. **Adzooma** – https://www.adzooma.com

AI-Driven Analytics & Insights

1. **Google Analytics 4 (GA4)** – https://analytics.google.com
2. **Tableau AI** – https://www.tableau.com
3. **Crimson Hexagon** – https://www.crimsonhexagon.com